That the 'culture' of an organization is crucial to its performance is now widely recognized, but theoretical frameworks for the understanding of organizational culture are still poorly developed. Complex analytical problems are often trivialized by the promise of a quick management fix. Too often, studies of organizational culture are conceived from a management perspective, and deal largely with problems of leadership. Professor Alvesson's wideranging book offers, in contrast, a sophisticated overview of the various issues which a theory of organizational culture must address. A recognized authority, he provides a subtle, critical account of contemporary theoretical approaches in the field. Specialists will be particularly interested in his treatment of the problem of cultural – or culturally constructed – ambiguity in management structures and procedures, and in his sober evaluation of the large claims of the critical cultural studies movement. The book can also be used as an introductory text by all those who require an authoritative, critical, and up-to-date account of this increasingly influential field.

CULTURAL PERSPECTIVES ON ORGANIZATIONS

CULTURAL PERSPECTIVES
ON ORGANIZATIONS

MATS ALVESSON

University of Gothenburg

Published by the Press Syndicate of the University of Cambridge
The Pitt Building, Trumpington Street, Cambridge CB2 1RP
40 West 20th Street, New York, NY 10011–4211, USA
10 Stamford Road, Oakleigh, Victoria 3166, Australia

© Cambridge University Press 1993

First published 1993

Printed in Great Britain at the University Press, Cambridge

A catalogue record for this book is available from the British Library

Library of Congress cataloguing in publication data
Alvesson, Mats, 1956–
Cultural perspectives on organizations / Mats Alvesson.
p.   cm.
Includes bibliographical references.
ISBN 0 521 40136 4
1. Corporate culture. 2. Culture. 3. Organizational behavior.
I. Title.
HD58.7.A473 1993
302.3′5 – dc20 92–37770 CIP

ISBN 0 521 401364 hardback

Contents

Preface

My interest in organizational culture dates from 1983 and was first directed towards trying to understand the enormous popularity of the field. Having just completed a dissertation entitled 'Organization Theory and Technocratic Consciousness', I was well prepared to look at the field with a critical eye. I later became more 'positively' interested in its concepts, theories, and general approach to an understanding of organizational life. This led to some empirical projects, and in the course of time the initial critical approach cultivated by my bias towards the critical theory of the Frankfurt school was complemented by more interpretive studies. A certain disappointment with much of what has been achieved in the field inspired this attempt to encourage a more reflective understanding of culture in organization research by challenging some of the assumptions and foci of mainstream studies.

Parts of this book draw upon material which has been published elsewhere. Some sections of chapters 2 and 3 are based on 'The Culture Perspectives on Organizations: Instrumental Values and Basic Features of Culture' (*Scandinavian Journal of Management* 5: 123–36) and 'Concepts of Organizational Culture and Presumed Links to Efficiency' (*Omega* 17: 323–33), and chapter 4 borrows from 'On Focus in Cultural Studies of Organizations' (*Scandinavian Journal of Management* 2: 105–20). I am grateful to Pergamon Press for permission to use this material.

A number of colleagues have read and commented upon earlier drafts; I thank Leif Borgert, Dennis Mumby, Linda Putnam, and Kaj Sköldberg, as well as Barbara Czarniawska-Joerges, Mark Eads, Claes Edlund, Sten Jönsson, Rolf Lundin, Joanne Martin, and Howard Schwartz. I also appreciate the advice of three anonymous reviewers consulted by Cambridge University Press. I am grateful to Inga Collin, Ann McKinnon, and Margareta Samuelsson for valuable administrative assistance and to Barbara Metzger for editing the manuscript.

Introduction

This book deals with the why and how of cultural studies of organizations. Broadly speaking, it identifies weaknesses in current approaches and suggests novel ways of making us more alert to the possibilities of cultural analysis, showing how it can lead to interesting interpretations of organizations and working life. The general aim is thus to contribute to a more reflective mode of research in this field.

A glance at even a few works that use the term 'organizational culture' will reveal enormous variation in the definitions of this term and even more in the use of the term 'culture'. 'Culture' has no fixed or broadly agreed meaning even in anthropology (Ortner, 1984), but variation in its use is especially noticeable in organizational culture studies, partly because of the substantial variation in the purpose and depth of these studies. In addition there is the fact that organizational culture is studied by researchers from various disciplines – for example, management, communication, sociology, psychology, anthropology, and folklore – and with research orientations ranging from the positivistic to the interpretive and the post-modernist. Finally, the concept of culture seems to lend itself to very different understandings of its meaning – for example, as collectively shared forms of cognition, values, meanings, beliefs, understandings, ideologies, rules, norms, symbols, emotions, expressiveness, the unconscious, behaviour patterns, structures, practices, etc. – all of which may be made targets of study.

Perhaps the most important cause of this variation, however, is the philosophical and meta-theoretical assumptions that guide approaches to organizational culture studies. The most important distinction is between an objectivist–functionalist view of social reality and social science and a subjectivist, interpretive approach (Burrell & Morgan, 1979; Smircich, 1983a). Widely differing views on the ontological status of culture – its relation to the basic nature of social reality – and how to attain knowledge of it result in very different understandings of culture that are only to a limited extent reflected in differences in its formal definition. Definitions do not tell us much about complicated topics,

1

and one and the same definition can be used by writers with very different orientations. As Ricoeur (1978: 137) has put it, 'words have actual meanings only in a sentence and lexical entities – words in the dictionary – have only potential meanings'. To say, for example, that culture is 'a set of shared values, beliefs, meanings, and understandings' gives some hint of what we might mean by 'culture', but it does not limit the ways in which we can use the term. Further definitions seldom succeed in giving such concepts any crystal-clear meaning.

These differences in research purposes and interests, definitions and foci, and philosophical foundations of inquiry make it impossible to talk about organizational culture as a well-defined, coherent area of study. That certain researchers are interested in 'culture' does not mean that they have very much in common. It could therefore be advocated that in many cases the term should be abandoned in favour of some slightly more precise (and less contested) term such as 'organizational climate', 'corporate ideology', 'informal behaviour patterns', 'norm system', or 'shared system of symbols and meanings'. The term 'culture' might be seen not as corresponding to any particular empirical object but simply as a way of thinking about social reality.

In this book I use the term 'organizational culture' as an umbrella concept for academic studies which take a serious interest in cultural and symbolic phenomena. This term directs the spotlight in a particular direction rather than mirroring a concrete reality for possible study. I am in considerable sympathy with Frost *et al.*'s (1985: 17) 'definition' of organizational culture: 'Talking about organizational culture seems to mean talking about the importance for people of symbolism – of rituals, myths, stories and legends – and about the interpretation of events, ideas, and experiences that are influenced and shaped by the groups within which they live.' This position is in line with the view broadly shared by many modern anthropologists (e.g. D'Andrade, 1984; Geertz, 1973). I will also, however, take organizational culture to include values and assumptions about social reality.

Most of the diverse perspectives surveyed here share, at least to some extent, many of the following assumptions about cultural phenomena: that they are related to history and tradition, have some depth, are difficult to grasp and account for, and must be interpreted; that they are collective and shared by members of groups and primarily ideational in character, having to do with values, understandings, beliefs, knowledge, and other intangibles; and that they are holistic and subjective rather than strictly rational and analytical (Hofstede *et al.*, 1990). Löfgren (1982) suggests that different definitions of culture can be seen as shifting analytical perspectives which can illuminate different aspects of cultural processes and conditions.

Viewing culture broadly as a shared and learned world of experiences, meanings, values, and understandings which inform people and which are expressed, reproduced, and communicated partly in symbolic form is consistent with a variety of approaches to the conduct of concrete studies.

Background to the current interest in organizational culture

Organizational culture research long pre-dates the 'corporate-culture boom' of the past decade, but since 1980 a broader and more consistent interest in it has emerged. The reasons for this increased interest are various. For many writers it arises from theoretical concerns (see, e.g. Frost *et al.*, 1985). Traditional organization research, often objectivist and abstract, has proved incapable of providing deep, rich, and realistic pictures of the objects of study, and the dominance of quantitative, hypothesis-testing studies has discouraged alternative approaches. Many researchers seem to have experienced this situation as an intellectual straitjacket. Systems and contingency theory as well as other functionalist approaches have been targets of broad attacks, some of which have advocated a cultural approach to organizations and the use of qualitative methods such as ethnography. The culture concept also has the theoretical advantage that it seems to provide a conceptual bridge between micro- and macro-levels of analysis and between organizational behaviour and strategic management (Smircich, 1983a: 346).

Furthermore, as Smircich remarks, everyone intuitively 'knows' what culture means or at least that it is important. (Unfortunately, this easily creates problems in connection with theoretical precision.) Culture is closely related to lived experience and is therefore popular. People seem to like to talk about culture. The word is also economical: one word signifies a broad range of intangible societal and organizational phenomena. It is a word for the lazy.

A general interest in societal culture issues (at least in the Swedish context) has accompanied recent rapid cultural change in or associated with such areas as sex roles, sexuality, morality, the prolongation of youth, internationalization and immigration. As cultural patterns become more diverse and less stable, the relative character of culture becomes more obvious, and this general background has probably affected the interest in culture in management and working life (Alvesson & Berg, 1992).

Increased emphasis on consumption and hedonism in certain Western societies has reduced the impact of traditional authoritarian leadership, obedience, Protestant work morale and motivation and inspired the development of new, 'softer' means of controlling people (Lasch, 1978; Ziehe & Stubenrauch, 1982). Again, in affluent societies a set of motives broader than the traditional material ones of pay and employment seems to be important to workers, and the culture concept offers the possibility of a more successful approach to this development.

The productivity problems of Western societies, especially the USA may have provided a more distinct material basis for the exploration of new ideas. Japanese success appears to have some connection with Japanese 'corporate cultures', and this has suggested to many that the concept may have something to offer. Changes in production technology and/or work organization may also have been important in bringing the cultural dimension into sharper focus. Deal and Kennedy (1982) refer to the motivational benefits of small units and the development of information technology which has facilitated decentralization and made control possible without various intermediate levels between top management and operative units. Culture then becomes significant as a glue holding the organization together, a soft complement to hard data. Brulin (1989) suggests that efforts to reduce storage costs by increasing the through-put speed of products in manufacturing processes call for greater flexibility and a higher degree of commitment from the workforce than in traditional forms of work organization. Beckérus, Edström *et al.* (1988) call attention to changes in production technology which allow for more flexible production patterns, a greater degree of market orientation, and changes in values and life-styles among employees and in society as tending to make corporate control more complicated and efforts to involve workers in the company more significant. While this does not necessarily lead to an interest in corporate culture, it creates a background for it.

The emergence of new forms of organization has also helped to make the cultural dimension more salient. In this regard, Kunda and Barley (1988) stress the expansion of high-tech companies employing a large number of professionals whose loyalty is crucial, and I have made a similar proposal (Alvesson, 1993 a, b). Weick (1987: 118) speaks of a reduction in the number of mechanistic organizations and a corresponding increase in the proportion of organic organizations 'held together by culture'. 'This is why we see more culture and judge it to be more important. There is not more culture, there simply are more organic systems.' The important trend away from mass production to service and information in the economy makes ideational aspects – the regulation of beliefs and images – more important, for example, in service management (Alvesson, 1990). Associated with this is a change in emphasis from control of behaviour and measurement of outputs to control of employees' attitudes and commitment, the latter being crucial for the employee service-mindedness which in turn determines the level of customer satisfaction.

Both Van Maanen and Barley (1985) and Alvesson and Berg (1992) have suggested that organizations these days do not automatically produce 'enough' local culture – naturally emerging, distinct organization-wide cultural patterns – and it is this which accounts for current interest in it. Van Maanen and Barley remark that it is because modern management methods are antithetical to 'cultural authority' that 'the notion of "organizational culture" has attained a faddish appeal in business literature' (p. 40).

The increasing interest in organizational culture is to some extent a consequence of the way in which the idea is marketed. Consultants, described by Czarniawska-Joerges (1988a) as 'merchants of meaning', are especially important here. Burrell (1992: 87) describes them as 'seeking to provide the expensive but quick fix to an industrial and commercial audience who, ever hungry for novelty, are eager to consume different ideas before turning greedily to a newer fad in the relentless pursuit of busyness'. The management consultancy company McKinsey, for example, sponsored the best-selling books of Peters and Waterman (1982) and Deal and Kennedy (1982), apparently in order to improve its market position against competitors such as the Boston Consulting Group.

In summary, the recent interest in organizational culture can be understood variously as a response to frustration over the dominance of positivistic approaches in American organization theory, a strategy for confronting the marketing problems of management consultants, and a by-product of technological, social, and organizational change. These determinants point in different directions: the theoretical ones are very different from the commercial ones and both from those arising from change in organizational forms. At the same time, new empirical phenomena of course inspire new theoretical approaches and new consultancy approaches (or marketing strategies). The average academic writings on organizational culture have become increasingly 'practitioner-friendly' (Barley, Meyer, & Gash, 1988). The concept of organizational culture will vary depending on one's point of view – for example, that of an open-minded observer (such as Weick, 1987) identifying an organic organization which cannot be managed by traditional bureaucratic means, that of a consultant or pragmatically oriented academic eager to propose a new solution with a broad range of possibilities, or that of an interpretive academic interest in a new theoretical view rather than a particular research object or practical problem. These differences are not always clear-cut; elements of the various perspectives and interests often overlap, creating a messy collection of intellectual streams crudely subsumed in the concept of organizational culture. An understanding of organizational culture – and of the various orientations within the field – demands some awareness of its background and of the various rationales for talking about it at all.

Objectives

One of this book's main objectives is to consider why we should conduct cultural studies of organizations – specifically, what knowledge-constitutive or cognitive interests (Habermas, 1972) make such studies worthwhile. In principle there are two broad answers. The first views organizational culture as a means of promoting more effective managerial action, whereas the second views culture as a point of entry for a broader understanding of and critical reflection upon organizational life and work. These two answers are not necessarily mutually exclusive (understanding and reflection may precede effective action), but the goal of promoting effectiveness tends to rule out complicated research designs and 'deep' thinking, while promotion of broad critical reflection presupposes that the project is not subordinated to managerial interests.

The first approach – the more common but also the more debatable – proceeds from the assumption that culture is in some way related to organizational performance. Advocates of this view believe that it is vital to uncover linkages or causal relationships between the two and to produce knowledge that increases the chance of affecting cultural phenomena (symbols, rites, values, norms, etc.) or cultural systems in their totality, so that outcomes considered beneficial can be attained. This is an 'offensive' formulation of the issue, one which suggests that culture is a tool or guiding concept for achieving effectiveness. A 'defensive' version of the culture-performance link sees culture more as an obstacle to economic rationality and effectiveness, and it then becomes a question of controlling culture so that it does not obstruct rational plans or intentions based, for example, on strategic thinking or financial criteria. In other words, this defensive interest in culture is motivated by a desire to avoid difficulties in companies due to the 'negative' features of culture such as resistance to change and cultural conflicts. While the offensive view can be described as a *tool view* of culture, the defensive view can be called a *trap view*.

The second approach assumes that a rich, complex, holistic understanding of the workplace will make it easier to appreciate both the positive and the negative features of organizational life and help to counteract the taken-for-granted beliefs and values which limit personal autonomy. From this perspective, cultural studies provide insight into organizational life which may contribute to freeing thought from its traditional patterns. Thus, the purpose of cultural studies becomes liberating human potential or, more defensively, illuminating the obstacles of emancipation – ideas, values, and understandings of social arrangements that are generally thought of as natural but are in fact socially constructed and susceptible to change. The task of cultural studies, then, is to encourage critical reflection on beliefs, values, and understandings of social conditions.

Not all researchers would be prepared to endorse either of these two approaches. Many seem to prefer a more general and perhaps more cautious position stressing the development of knowledge or interpretation without any clear purpose. The primary task is often identified as exploring organizations as a subjective experience; understanding is viewed as an end in itself rather than being tied to either technical problem-solving or emancipation. This general understanding may, however, be 'used' in different ways which normally touch upon one or the other of these approaches broadly understood. Understanding – when experienced as important – may either encourage new forms of instrumental action or make people feel more enlightened.

The other major objective of this book is to stimulate reflection on how cultural studies of organization can best be conducted. The question here is not one of method or technique but one of conceptualization of the research object. What does it mean to see an organization as a culture? The following issues seem to me significant for contemporary organizational culture research: (1) the role and meaning of metaphors for both organizations and culture; (2) the significance of culture for corporate performance; (3) the potential of cultural studies as a counterweight to ethnocentrism and parochialism and thereby as a facilitator of reflection on self-limiting forms of understanding; (4) the relative importance for organizational culture studies of 'substantive', materially based social practice as opposed to ideational phenomena; (5) the question of level of analysis – whether the organization is a culture, a set of subcultures, or a local reflection of societal macro-culture (a societal subculture); and (6) integration, contradiction, and ambiguity. Some of these issues – for example, culture in relation to parochialism, materialism, and societal culture – are absent from the agenda of mainstream research,[1] and others receive far too little attention. Careful consideration of each of these themes will highlight the weaknesses and strengths of various approaches and suggest improvements that may help organizational culture research to produce broad, comprehensive interpretations of organizations and working life.

This book is an effort to clarify alternative approaches to organizational culture, to contribute to an increased awareness of the phenomena that cultural studies of organizations address, to facilitate 'better' choices in the development of cultural perspectives, and to encourage attention to different aspects of traditional objects of study – in short, to contribute to a more sensitive use of the idea of culture in organization and management studies.

Notes

1 The heterogeneity of the literature in this field makes it difficult to generalize about it, and I am well aware that many contributors to it are 'not guilty' of this charge. My critique is directed mainly at the research typically conducted in the business schools and university management departments which dominate the field. The work of sociologists, anthropologists, and students of communication is to a lesser degree also a target.

ONE

Culture as metaphor and metaphors for culture

Metaphors have been the subject of increasing attention in recent years, both in social science in general and organizational analysis in particular. Metaphors are seen as important organizing devices in thinking and talking about complex phenomena. The discovery of culture in organization theory has contributed to this interest, as many researchers have come to see culture as a new metaphor for organization with a considerable potential for developing new ideas and new forms of understanding.

Below I will discuss the distinction indicated in the title of this chapter exploring the metaphor concept and calling for more reflection upon the metaphors that are used for culture, I argue that culture should not be seen as the 'final' image to be used when organizations (or particular organizational phenomena) are being conceptualized. Instead we have good reason to investigate and reflect upon metaphors for culture (i.e. a metaphor for the metaphor) in organizational culture research.

The metaphor concept

It was once thought that, whereas metaphors were useful and necessary in poetry and rhetoric, the precision of science demanded literal expressions and well-defined words. Many people even today adhere to this view (e.g. Pinder & Bourgeois, 1982), which Tsoukas (1991) calls the 'metaphors-as-dispensable-literary devices' perspective. More commonly, however, metaphors are recognized as vital for understanding social research (and language use in general) and as a necessary element in creativity and the development of new approaches to research objects.

A metaphor is created when a term is transferred from one system or level of meaning to another, thereby illuminating central aspects of the latter and shadowing others. A metaphor allows an object to be perceived and understood from the viewpoint of another object. It thus creates a departure from literal meaning: 'a word receives a metaphorical meaning in specific contexts within which they are opposed to other words taken literally; this shift in meaning results mainly from a clash between literal meanings, which excludes literal use of the word in question' (Ricoeur, 1978: 138). A good metaphor depends on an appropriate mix of similarity and difference between the transferred word and the focal one. Where there is too much or too little similarity or difference, the point may not be understood.

In a narrow, traditional sense, a metaphor is simply an *illustrative device*; thus words which make language richer or more felicitous and formal models can both be regarded as metaphors (Brown, 1976). In a very broad sense, in contrast, all knowledge is metaphorical in that it emerges from or is 'constructed' from some point of view. So, too, are our experiences, for 'our ordinary conceptual system, in terms of which we both think and act, is fundamentally metaphorical in nature' (Lakoff & Johnson, 1980: 3). Metaphor can thus be seen as *a crucial element in how people relate to reality*. This has implications for our understanding of everyday life as well as our understanding of science. Empirical 'data' do not speak directly to the researcher; they are partly determined by metaphors drawing attention to various aspects of the research object. In terms of theoretical frameworks we can talk about a *root metaphor* which is a fundamental image of the world on which one is focusing, and an *organizing metaphor* (Mangham & Overington, 1987) which frames and structures a more limited part of reality.

Brown (1976) points to some of the characteristics of metaphors as follows: Metaphors involve what Aristotle called 'giving the thing a name that belongs to something else'. If a metaphor is taken literally, it usually appears absurd. The necessary ingredient of difference has a specific cognitive function: 'it makes us stop in our tracks and examine it. It offers us a new awareness' (p. 173). Metaphors are intended to be understood; 'they are category errors with a purpose, linguistic madness with a method' (p. 173). Metaphors must be approached and understood as if they were true at the same time that we are aware that they are fictitious – created and artificial.

From a traditional scientific point of view, the problem with metaphors is that they cannot be translated into more precise, objective language and thus elude rigorous measurement and testing. As Sennett (1980: 78) puts it, 'a metaphor creates a meaning greater than the sum of its parts, because the parts interact'. The metaphorical usage of words involves fantasy and associations which bring them generative power but limit their appropriateness for empiricists. Pinder and Bourgeois (1982: 647) admit that metaphors and tropes cannot altogether be avoided but worry about their uncontrolled, even deliberate use in formal theory:

In short, because of the impossibility of avoiding metaphors and other tropes in everyday language, they are bound to play a role in the early stages of inquiry, guiding speculations in a heuristic manner. But the ideal of scientific precision is literal language, so, to the extent that it is possible, administrative science must strive to control figurative terms in the development of formal hypothesis and theory. The point at which a trope loses its heuristic value and starts to mislead research and theory construction is difficult to determine. Therefore it is important to formulate concepts in literal terms that are rooted in observable organizational phenomena as soon as possible during the development of ideas into theory.

This argument proceeds, however, from the assumption that 'objective reality' can be perceived and evaluated on its own terms. Instead, all perception is guided by conceptualization of the object through a *gestalt* created by metaphorical thinking; it is impossible to let the 'objective data' speak for themselves (Brown, 1976; Morgan, 1983). According to Brown (1976: 178), 'the choice for sociology is not between scientific rigor as against poetic insight. The choice is rather between more or less fruitful metaphors, and between using metaphors or being their victims.'[1]

Mastery of the metaphors involved in thinking and research may encourage creativity and provide insight (Czarniawska-Joerges, 1988a; Morgan, 1980; Schön, 1979). It also draws attention to the partiality of the understanding gained by an approach built on a particular root metaphor and may foster tolerance for alternative approaches. Beyond this, it may facilitate examination of the basic assumptions of a particular conceptualization of a phenomenon; the *gestalt* of the research object may prove to be different from what the definitions and rhetoric suggest. Many authors writing on culture have adopted a new vocabulary which indicates a more interpretive, anthropological orientation, but the language used is often misleading. As Calàs and Smircich (1987: 18) put it, commenting on mainstream organization culture studies, 'those who comprise the *Corporate Culture* theme have done an excellent job of staying within "positive/ functionalist" assumptions while using the rhetoric of "myth", "rituals", and "qualitative methods"'. Attention to the metaphor concept (as root metaphor or organizing concept) might encourage a deeper, more sceptical and reflective perception of what people mean by culture. In this critical and reflective task it is not so much explicit metaphors as the 'old', implicit ones – sometimes called 'dead' metaphors – that are the objects of interest.[2]

Metaphors – some problems

Despite the benefits that the use of metaphors appears to offer the study of organizations (see, e.g., Berg, 1982; Mangham & Overington, 1987; Morgan,

1980, 1986), it also presents some problems. One of these is the risk of using 'bad' ones. An appealing metaphor may stand in the way of a less elegant but more accurate and elaborate description. For example, the garbage-can metaphor for organizational decision-making (March & Olsen, 1976) may have more rhetorical appeal than theoretical value (Pinder & Bourgeois, 1982).[3] The degree of overlap between the type of decision-making process addressed and the garbage can is too small; key features of the garbage can – its bad smell, its containing material packed together that is considered refuse – seem of limited relevance (see Pinder & Bourgeois, 1982). This problem basically concerns the level of expression and not so much the root metaphor (and other metaphors guiding thought) itself. As Tsoukas (1991: 32) remarks, the garbage-can metaphor is 'simply a figure of speech, a literary illustration to make sense of organisational decision-making and not a metaphor intended directly to reveal formal identities between garbage cans and organisations'. The metaphor does not necessarily have to be explicitly addressed, which would avoid the problem. March and Olsen could, for example, have conducted their analysis without referring to the garbage can and kept their metaphor to themselves.

A related difficulty is the 'catchiness' problem which springs partly from the current popularity of metaphors in organization studies. This can easily lead to the excessive use of seductive metaphorical expressions, rather than the development of theoretical metaphors that really do shed new light on things. As in the case of culture, the very popularity of metaphors can make it 'too easy' to play with them, which in turn can lead to superficiality. We can thus talk about a 'fashion problem' as regards metaphors in contemporary organization theory.

A third problem, once again related to the others, concerns the risk of a supermarket attitude to metaphors. (I am now redirecting the focus somewhat and referring to metaphors in the sense of analytic devices or root metaphors rather than 'merely' as expressions or labels.) There is the risk that focusing on the metaphorical level will draw attention away from the deeper or more basic levels of social research, such as the paradigmatic assumptions on which metaphors rely (on these various levels, see Morgan, 1980). For example, Morgan's (1986) *Images of Organization*, while a valuable contribution in many regards, may convey the impression that the more metaphors are employed the more comprehensive the understanding of organizational phenomena (Reed, 1990). Instead, mastery of a particular perspective demands complete understanding of its paradigmatic roots and their existential and political aspects (on the relationship between metaphors and politics, see Tinker, 1986). Attempting to employ more than a few guiding concepts in advanced analysis results in superficiality. A fourth problem concerns the oversimplifications that can follow, if too much emphasis is put on some particular gestalt (metaphor, image) which is seen as guiding and summarizing the research approach. It is unlikely that the metaphors employed (espoused) will always illuminate the researchers' basic view (*gestalt*) of the phenomenon. Complex understanding is perhaps more often derived from a synthesis of different metaphors than from a single sharp-profile picture. This problem arises partly from the limitations of current metaphors and partly from the complexity of the phenomena we deal with. For example, it is unlikely that any researcher sees an organization exclusively as a machine or exclusively as an organism or even exclusively as a combination of the two, and the addition of further metaphors to 'capture' the framework may simply obscure and distort it; thinking and analysis are not the same as the aggregation of metaphorical bits. There is also the problem that language is restricted. The words which we have at our disposal do not always adequately signify just what we want to pin-point.

We have already noted that the advantage of metaphors is that at one and the same time they illuminate and hide aspects of a particular phenomenon. We must remember that the reductionistic element in using metaphors not only concerns metaphors in relation to research objects; it also affects efforts to make sense of research and to develop frameworks. Saying that organization researchers treat their object of study as if it were a machine or an organism certainly illuminates some important aspects of the treatment of the object, but at the same time draws attention away from others. The reductionism of this enterprise is justifiable as long as the aspects illuminated are important and interesting and the reductionism is recognized. My impression is that at the theory/research-object interface this is generally the case but that discussion of theory and the frameworks that guide researchers (the theory/meta-theory interface) could benefit from more explicit consideration of this issue.

These problems are not of course arguments against the use of metaphors. Rather, they point to the need for an approach that is self-critical and reflective, avoiding the temptation to overuse metaphors and reminding oneself and the reader that they do not tell the whole story.

Culture as critical variable versus culture as root metaphor

In a classic overview of concepts of culture in organizational analysis, Smircich (1983a) has distinguished between culture as a variable and culture as a root metaphor. Researchers who see culture as a variable draw upon a more traditional, objectivist, and functionalist view of social reality and try to improve models of organization by taking sociocultural subsystems, in addition to traditionally recognized variables, into account. In contrast, researchers who see culture as a root metaphor approach organizations as if they were cultures and draw upon anthropology in developing radically new theories or paradigms.

Researchers who treat culture as a variable recognize that organizations produce or are accompanied by more or less distinct cultural traits, such as values, norms, rituals, ceremonies, and verbal expression, and that these features affect the behaviour of managers and employees. Many writers have argued that organizational culture contributes to the systemic balance and effectiveness of an organization. The idea that a 'strong corporate culture' has a distinct and positive impact on performance (e.g., Deal & Kennedy, 1982; Peters & Waterman, 1982) is still very popular, but during the 1980s it seems to have become increasingly common to examine the relevance of culture to organizational change. The improvement of organizational performance was increasingly viewed as partly a matter of achieving planned cultural change (e.g., Wilkins & Patterson, 1985). Managing culture is frequently equated with changing culture.

The proponents of this view suggest that the positive functions fulfilled by culture (in the sense of shared values and beliefs) include providing a sense of identity to members of the organization, facilitating commitment to a larger whole (the organization, its purpose, or whatever), enhancing system stability, and serving as a sense-making device which can guide and shape behaviour, motivating employees to do the 'right' things (Smircich, 1983a). The question is 'how to mold and shape internal culture in particular ways and how to change culture, consistent with managerial purposes' (p. 346). Culture is viewed, then, as interesting in the search for suitable means of control and improved management. Ideas about causality are crucial here; culture change is expected to have recognizable effects on important outputs such as loyalty, productivity, and perceived quality of service.

Instead of considering culture something that an organization has, researchers proceeding from the root-metaphor idea stress that the organization is a culture or, rather, can be seen as if it were a culture: 'Culture as a root metaphor promotes a view of organizations as expressive forms, manifestations of human consciousness. Organizations are understood and analyzed not mainly in economic or material terms, but in terms of their expressive, ideational, and symbolic aspects' (p. 348). According to this perspective, 'organizational culture is not just another piece of the puzzle, it is the puzzle' (Pacanowsky & O'Donnell-Trujillo, 1983: 146). Therefore, the research agenda is to explore organization as 'subjective experience' (Smircich, 1983a). The mode of thought that underlies the idea of culture as a root metaphor is hermeneutical or phenomenological rather than objectivist. The social world is seen not as objective, tangible, and measurable but as constructed by people and reproduced by the networks of symbols and meanings that unite people and make shared action possible (Burrell & Morgan, 1979; Putnam, 1983).

Advocates of the root-metaphor view of culture are inclined to play down the pragmatic results that can help management increase effectiveness in favour of more general understanding and reflection as the major emphasis of cultural studies. In principle, for them nothing is 'not culture', and therefore culture cannot be related to anything else. (Of course, different elements of culture can be related to each other.) Not all proponents of the root-metaphor view strictly conform to this theoretical ideal, but even those who make room in their analyses for 'non-cultural' phenomena or aspects tend to avoid explicitly relating them to culture.

Smircich's distinction has been vital in framing views on organizational culture and cultural studies. It points to crucial differences in basic assumptions that are not necessarily clear from a superficial reading of texts. There are, however, some problems with it. First, whereas some researchers very clearly adhere to a traditional understanding of organizations, explicitly discussing variables, 'measuring' culture, and so on, and others fully accept and proceed from a culture metaphor and focus exclusively on symbolism and meanings, many do not easily fit into either category. A rather large number of researchers fall between the two, refraining from reducing culture to a variable without fully viewing an organization as a culture. The problem is well illustrated by Smircich (1983a) herself; many of the works she cites appear in both 'variable' and 'metaphor' sections of her overview.

Part of this classification problem is that cultural concepts – values, rites, rituals, tales, etc. – do not readily lend themselves to quantification or to strict variable thinking, and consequently, even researchers not strongly oriented to the root-metaphor position often adopt a qualitative approach. This weakens the 'variable' bias, even among those interested in pragmatic results and predictions, and who adhere to traditional ontology and epistemology. At the other extreme, taking culture as a root metaphor leaves little room for aspects other than symbols and meanings; but organizations are normally economic entities in which material conditions, external environment, competition, and performance – dimensions not well captured by a cultural perspective – must be included. The culture-as-root-metaphor approach has interesting things to say about traditional issues such as strategy (Smircich & Stubbart, 1985), technology (Berg, 1985b), or business concept (Alvesson, 1993a), phenomena which the proponents of a variable approach would not put in a 'culture subsystem box,' but there are other important aspects which are difficult to include in a cultural analysis. Consequently, many researchers who treat culture as a metaphor also address 'non-cultural' aspects. Working strictly with culture as a root metaphor may lead to the reduction of everything to symbolism,[4] and therefore many researchers combine cultural and other understandings.

Another problem of classification is that researchers who see culture as a variable do not use cultural concepts in a literal way; here culture itself must be seen as metaphorical. For example, 'variable metaphors' for corporate culture could be tool, obstacle, or control mechanism. Such metaphors are, of course, limited in scope, illuminating not a major part of an organization but a restricted set of human (managerial) functions. They may or may not be subordinated to another, more basic (root) metaphor, such as a machine, organism, or system, or no particular root metaphor – in the sense of a theoretically coherent *gestalt* or image – may be used. In this last case, culture and other subsystems are then seen as comprising an aggregate of components, which are treated without reference back to a particular distinct root metaphor. Here, too, the basic view of conceptualization of an organization is of course metaphorical (as is all knowledge), but the fact remains that the project is not guided by any particular *gestalt* created by the comparison of an organization with something else.

Finally, a more modest use of the culture concept which still informs a substantial part of an analysis of an organization falls between the root-metaphor and variable view. This view takes culture as an organizing metaphor which guides thinking and analysis in a more restricted way (see, e.g., Allaire & Firsirotu, 1984; Schein, 1985; Whipp, Rosenfeld, & Pettigrew, 1989).

Metaphors for culture

The use of culture as an organizing metaphor in fact implies 'metaphorization' at many levels. Not only does organizational culture, i.e. the combination and juxtaposition of organization and culture, create a metaphor, but the word culture is also metaphorical in itself. Culture is not a literal word; it draws in turn on another metaphor. Thus, we can go even further and look at *the metaphor behind the metaphor*. When people talk about culture in organization studies, for example, what do they think of? What are their *gestalts*? Is culture seen as 'personality writ large', 'an overall control mechanism', 'a community' or what? Culture defined as a set of shared values, for example, can be used in all these senses. (Further definitions of 'values' do not necessarily restrict the possibilities.) If proponents of culture as a metaphor (such as Smircich and Morgan) are correct, not only the conceptualization of organization but also the conceptualization of metaphor is metaphorical. And it is so irrespective of whether culture is used as a root or an organizing metaphor.

The idea then is to determine which are the metaphors that structure culture, making an image of it. I will not distinguish here between root metaphors and the more modest forms of organizing metaphor, but will treat them together. A particular metaphor or metaphorical expression can be used in different ways as organizing or root metaphors. For example, organizational culture understood as a paradigm shared by organizational members can refer either to a subsystem of cognition (a 'soft' variable) which can facilitate or obstruct strategic change (another 'soft' variable), or to an all-embracing view of an organizational reality (root metaphor), which could mean, for example, that strategic change is seen as paradigmatic change and not as something 'outside' the paradigm. The metaphorical nature of culture and paradigm is thus the same.

Interpreting the metaphor behind the metaphor is an uncertain and difficult business. It is seldom self-evident how the former should be conceptualized. It is by no means always possible to find a particular *gestalt* or image created by the juxtaposition of culture and something else. The multidimensionality of what 'culture' refers to often prevents us from seeing it as a gestalt, or from using a single phrase or meaning (combination of words) to capture the metaphor involved. The problem is partly linguistic: the capacity of language to signify is limited. This restriction should remind us that the full complexity involved is seldom illuminated by invoking a metaphor. Rather, the metaphor draws attention to certain central features in thinking about the phenomenon. Metaphors are simplifications, not only of 'external' reality but also of research and thinking about 'reality'.

That the conceptualization of culture is itself metaphorical has received very little attention in the organizational culture literature. Except for Nord (1985), who discusses social glue and magnet as metaphors for culture, few researchers have examined the metaphors they draw upon or create when they use culture as a theoretical concept. Strictly speaking, culture is too broad in itself and overlaps too closely with organization to be able to function as a metaphor. If we compare it with Brown's criteria for good metaphors as summarized earlier in this chapter, some doubts arise. It is not clear that it makes sense to view organizations 'as if' they were cultures. One could say that organizations, like societies, actually *are* cultures, i.e. organizations or collectives in organizations literally include or contain values, meanings, and symbols. Rather than pursue this aspect, I will simply point out that most researchers who successfully use a cultural approach by structuring culture in a particular way, actually produce the necessary 'as if qualities' and thus make possible the metaphor of organizational culture. In using a metaphor for culture, the culture concept is narrowed down and a clearer distance is created between it and organization. In order to clarify this idea it is necessary to extend the focus beyond organization and culture as the only elements creating the metaphor. The way in which culture is modified so that it also becomes a metaphor must be investigated. By looking at the metaphors used for (organizational) culture, we can better understand the guiding frameworks for organizational culture research.

Consideration of ten metaphors for culture drawn from the contemporary literature will reveal their differences and indicate some potential problems with particular uses of the culture concept in organization research.

Culture as exchange-regulator

One metaphor for culture is exchange-regulator. Culture is seen here as a control mechanism that can handle complex exchange relations. Wilkins and Ouchi (1983) 'take the paradigmatic view on culture and call it a clan' and define culture as 'shared social knowledge' (p. 469). Culture/clan is (1) a general paradigm that helps participants determine what is in the best interest of the collective and (2) the perception of goal congruence (the belief in a general or long-term equity) (p. 475). Their analysis suggests that complex exchange situations, characterized by ambiguity and difficulty in monitoring employees' performances, increase the risk of opportunistic behaviour (for arguments against this assumed connection see Alvesson & Lindkvist, 1993; Etzioni, 1988). Culture (clan) is for Wilkins and Ouchi a variable that can replace the need for close monitoring by socializing employees into believing that their objectives in the exchange process are congruent with those of the employed and by providing a general paradigm which facilitates the determination of what is best for the relationship. Culture provides members of the organization with intellectual tools and a 'long memory' which guarantee their perception and evaluation of fair rewards in the long run and thus discourage them from short-term opportunistic behaviour.

The culture variable, then, is viewed as a form of control which operates upon people's shared views on the utilitarian exchange relationship to reduce trans-action costs. Organizations in which a culture of the 'right kind' has been developed – by selective recruitment, socialization, and 'ceremonial control' (Ouchi, 1980) – will achieve high performance. Aspects of 'shared social knowledge' which are not directly relevant to exchange relations are neglected. For Wilkins and Ouchi culture has a specific and positive function.

Culture as compass

Another metaphor for culture in organizational research is the compass. Wiener (1988: 536), for example, draws attention to the direction-pointing capacity of the shared value system that he sees as the core of organizational culture:

> By definition, individual values serve as a guide to a person's intentions and actions. Similarly, organizational value systems provide guides for organizational goals, policies, and strategies. Thus, the nature of the values is a crucial factor in the impact that culture will have on organizational effectiveness. If the

prevailing values support appropriate goals and strategies, the culture is an important asset. Conversely, the wrong values can make the culture a major liability.

'Wrong' values are thus like a defective compass: they indicate the 'wrong' direction, and consequently people will not get where they want to go (or, perhaps, where management wants them to go). 'Right' values are associated with a well-functioning device and 'wrong' values with a defective one. Without suggesting that the compass metaphor captures the whole of Wiener's argument, it is possible to see it illuminating Wiener's distinctions between functional and elitist values and between traditions and charismatic leaders as sources of values. Functional values concern 'modes of conduct' and are useful for operations, while elitist values concern 'the status, superiority, and importance of the organization itself' (p. 537). In relation to the compass, these values parallel technical functionality and the image of the brand. Traditional values are anchored in history and are persistent, while leader-induced values are less stable. An idea of product durability and reliability apparently governs the argument, and the compass metaphor seems to throw some light on this. Wiener crosses types and sources of values and concludes, hardly surprisingly, that functional–traditional ones 'are most likely to contribute to the development of proper values and, consequently, to organizational effectiveness' (p. 538). These values are those which are long-lasting, reliable, relevant, and capable of keeping people on the right course.

Culture as social glue

Perhaps the most common view of culture is as social glue. The idea here is that organizations are integrated and controlled through informal, non-structural means – shared values, beliefs, understandings, and norms. Culture in this sense contributes to the avoidance of fragmentation, conflict, tension, and other miseries; organizational life is seen as characterized by consensus, harmony, community, and so on. There seem to be two major versions of the social-glue metaphor. One is more pragmatic and assumes that consensus and harmony are not only possible but also natural. This can be called the integration approach (Martin & Meyerson, 1988). Another version emphasizes the control aspect and, rather than postulating consensus as something organically produced, talks about corporate culture as a strategy for achieving social-glue-like effects. Ray (1986: 294) views corporate culture as the last frontier of control: 'the top management team aims to have individuals possess direct ties to the values and goals of the dominant élites in order to activate the emotion and sentiment which might lead to devotion, loyalty, and commitment to the company'. In this second version the glue is viewed as fragile, in need of maintenance work, and not always capable of holding the organization together.

Culture as sacred cow

Many researchers stress the deeper levels of culture and members' internalization of certain ideals and values, and the image of the sacred cow appears to capture significant dimensions of their approach. Gagliardi (1986), for example, speaks of the 'sacred' as significant for the core of culture. Crucial here are organizational values, which 'can be seen as the idealization of a collective experience of success in the use of a skill and the emotional transfiguration of previous beliefs' (p. 123). These values are the result of a historical process in which people gradually accept and internalize beliefs and values based on a leader's (often the founder's) 'vision' once it has been shown to be successful (see Schein, 1985). Through the idealization process, 'the rational acceptance of beliefs gives way to the emotional identification with values', which in due course become sacred. Gagliardi suggests that every organization has a primary strategy, the maintenance of its cultural identity, as distinct from a series of secondary strategies, derivative from the primary one, which are more explicit and tied to concrete objectives. This primary strategy is tightly coupled to the sacred values, and it places firm limits on change. Thus core values are seen as almost impossible to change because of their taken-for-granted character and the deep commitment to them of organizational members.

The sacred-cow metaphor for organizational culture thus stresses the limits of instrumental reason and focuses on deeper value commitments and the stability of the cultural core. The metaphor gives 'shared basic values' a different meaning from the compass or social glue even though the definitions of culture are sometimes similar. The sacred-cow view of course also can be seen as referring to similar functions as the compass or the social-glue idea – the metaphors are in no way contradictory – but it does not clearly show the direction of concrete behaviour, nor can it be regarded as a control strategy. Rather, what the sacred-cow metaphor refers to, controls strategies. It differs from others in referring to much deeper and more affective aspects of culture.

Culture as manager-controlled rites

Culture may also be seen as organizational rites which are (or can be) controlled by managers for instrumental purposes. Trice and Beyer (1985: 372) define 'rites' as 'organized and planned activities that have both practical and expressive consequences. The activities involved are usually relatively elaborate, dramatic, and consolidate various forms of cultural expression into one event, which is carried out through social interactions, usually for the benefit of an audience'. Although this definition suggests activities in tribal societies and rather complicated collective involvement, Trice and Beyer stress the possibilities for instrumental use (pp. 393–4):

> Rites thus clearly can be used to facilitate cultural change. To use them effectively, however, managers and others must recognize the rites and ceremonies already occurring around them and become aware of both their intended and latent consequences. With such an awareness, combined with a healthy respect for the power of the rites to help people maintain some sense of stability in the midst of change, managers can begin to use rites creatively and effectively to achieve desired cultural change.

This metaphor presumes that managers are capable of standing 'above' culture and controlling it, and it overlooks the possibility of considerable distance between the intent of a rite and the community's willingness to give it deep and lasting meaning (see Kunda, 1991).

Culture as affect-regulator

A quite different approach to culture concentrates on its affective and expressive dimensions. Van Maanen and Kunda (1989) emphasize that 'attempts to build, strengthen, deepen or thicken organizational culture often involve the subtle (or not so subtle) control of employee emotions – or at least those emotions expressed in the workplace' (p. 52) – and see culture as a 'control device' to 'inform, guide, and discipline the emotions of organizational members' (p. 56). For these researchers a core dimension of organizational life and what unites members and ties them to the organization is corporate socioaffective bonds. Attention may, alternatively, be focused on emotions of a more restricted nature, involving self-control and the reduction of tensions through socialization and certain types of symbols (see Dandridge, Mitroff, & Joyce, 1980).

Culture as non-order

The metaphor of non-order proceeds from the assumption that modern societies and organizations are characterized by ambiguity – uncertainty, contradiction, confusion – and that a cultural perspective on organizations must take this into account. This approach might even be seen as a negation of many common definitions of culture:

Cultural manifestations are not clearly consistent or clearly inconsistent with each other. Instead, the relationships between manifestations are characterized by a lack of clarity. Differences in interpretation are seen as incommensurable, irreconcilable, and unavoidable ... consensus, dissensus, and confusion coexist, making it difficult to draw cultural and subcultural boundaries. (Martin & Meyerson, 1988: 115, 117)

Some might object that this kind of situation suggests that no culture has yet been developed, but, as Martin (1987) remarks a modern, complex society or organization does not become 'non-cultural' because of fragmentation and differences in its social and cultural patterns.

Martin and Meyerson (1988) propose that rather than providing clarity and lucidity in a dark, formless jungle, culture can be seen as the jungle itself. This metaphor seems to me not very illuminating – most people probably associate it with lack of civilization and culture – but it is difficult to come up with something better. The concept of non-order may be the best choice to mark the non-systematic and contradictory character of cultural manifestations in organizations to which Martin and Meyerson draw attention. It contrasts nicely with prevailing ideas about the ordering and organizing functions of culture without suggesting that culture is absent.

Culture as blinders

Morgan (1986) has compared the organization to a 'psychic prison', and Krefting and Frost (1985) appeal to the same idea in speaking of 'blinders'. They argue that 'organizational culture is funneled through the unconscious' (p. 156) and therefore differs from what is indicated by the organization, which is a metaphor for order and orderliness.[5] Their understanding of organizational culture is inspired by Jungian ideas, which, although originally developed to explain individual development, have lately been extended to organizations. According to Krefting and Frost (p. 165),

Effective cultures need a balance, which requires the incorporation of shadows or other less dominant elements. Such cultures must also deal with 'problems posed by life-situations' (Turner) in complex and realistic ways rather than at the idealized, archetypal level. When organizational culture goes awry, blockage may well result from unincorporated shadows or unresolved archetypal conflicts; hence, exploring the problem in terms of shadows or archetypes may well be the way to approach it.

Viewing culture as being to a significant degree rooted in the unconscious leads to an emphasis on its deeper aspects: members have only limited access to it and easily become victims of shadows, archetypes, and fantasies. Any knowledge of it is likely to be uncertain and speculative (though perhaps very interesting).

Culture as world-closure

Another metaphor for culture that suggests that it prevents people from understanding social reality stresses sociological rather than psychological elements and may be called world-closure. The basic idea is that social reality is in principle open and negotiable; culture makes it appear given, natural, and, when it comes to basic premises, impossible (or at least very difficult) to question. This effect may be produced by traditions or other impersonal forces or by the more or less conscious influence of powerful actors using cultural and ideological means. Knights and Willmott (1987: 51–2), studying a British insurance company, interpret the chief executive's frequent use of the 'team' metaphor as follows:

> The use of the team metaphor involves activation of a number of interpretive schemes, facilities, and norms ... The notion of a team does not describe the situation – here, the assembly of Pensco's management. Rather, if successful, its articulation has the effect of *defining* the situation. In this case, its usage becomes symbolic and *ideological* in the sense that it draws upon this interpretive scheme to constitute the identity of Pensco middle management in a way that naturalizes, legitimizes, and thus reproduces prevailing asymmetries of power within (and beyond) the company ... The (widespread) appeal to the idea of a team conveys the image of a 'community' in which norms are shared, the objective of the 'game' is well established, the captain/leader speaks for the group, and the players are under a moral obligation to follow his instructions as they engage in the play.

Knights and Willmott see organizational culture as a management strategy which aims to implant management's favourable perceptions and definitions of social reality in the interpretive schemes of employees. If it is successful in this, these perceptions and definitions come to constitute a selective and biased world view that reproduces a particular social order and the asymmetrical representation of interests that characterizes it. As do some other metaphors examined here, this one places managers above cultural conditions, manipulating cultural elements rather than being shaped and/or restricted by culture.

Culture as dramaturgical domination

A closely related metaphor is dramaturgical domination. One of the most interesting examples of its application is Rosen's (1985), which emphasizes the manipulation of symbols and their dramatic character: 'social drama enacts the "reality" of a particular set of social relations through its public display (Moore & Myerhoff) under a set of conditions allowing a state of community to emerge, thus influencing consciousness in a manner likely to elicit consent' (p. 33). Social drama postulates social convention as natural and unquestionable. In dramas such as the one studied by Rosen – an annual breakfast for all managers and employees in an advertising agency – the particular form and content are the opposites of normal bureaucratic organizational conditions: instead of division of labour, hierarchy, exploitation, and frustration, the social drama transmits the notions of community, harmony, and unity. People are together, appear (almost) equal (normal status differences are minimized), and enjoy a moment of affluence and generosity from the company. The drama draws attention in a powerful way to features of the company that are highly atypical but become salient in the particular setting. Ceremonies of this type have 'doctrinal efficacy' in the sense that at relatively small cost (in time and money) they can contribute to culturally created, undoubtable reality (Rosen, 1985: 47). (It is, however, debatable how much impact situations of this kind normally have.) The dramaturgical-domination metaphor thus takes both symbolic and political aspects seriously. It notes the role of actors who manipulate symbolism and promote their interests, but it also illuminates the complexity of rites and ceremonies, portraying them as far more than mere tools or strategies.

Other metaphors for culture

These ten metaphors of course in no way exhaust the ways in which culture is used in organization research. The same guiding concept or framework can often be denoted in different ways, and beyond this there are many other approaches to culture which I will not attempt to illustrate. Additional examples of metaphors for culture in organizational analysis include contract (Jones, 1983), magnet (Nord, 1985), paradigm (Pfeffer, 1981), power game (Frost 1987), neurosis (Kets de Vries & Miller, 1986), hologram (Pondy, 1983, cited by Martin & Meyerson, 1988), island of clarity (Martin & Meyerson, 1988), and founder writ large (Martin, Sitkin, & Boehm, 1985) – the last two used somewhat sceptically.

Dimensions of contrast

There are many dimensions in which these various metaphors for organizational culture can be compared. I will indicate five of them here, and in doing so I have been to some extent inspired by Burrell and Morgan's (1979) distinction between objectivism and subjectivism and between regulative/consensual and radical/conflict assumptions.

The first dimension is functionalism versus non-functionalism. The functionalist position is that culture normally serves the common good – it promotes the effectiveness of the organization and the well-being of all its stakeholders. Opposition to this view may take several forms. The background and reproduction of culture is a complex affair, and cultural manifestations may include (non-functional) conflicts as well as consensus. Cultural manifestations can exist without fulfilling any positive function (being reproduced, for instance, by the autonomous powers of tradition). This position may be called the agnostic. Another position is that cultural manifestations serve the interests of the status quo and the ruling elite – they may be 'functional' for the elite but hardly for members in general. This view, held by Marxists and other proponents of critical theory, may be called the sectional functionalist. Yet another position is that culture is rooted in the unconscious, in traditions, and in other sources outside or in opposition to rational thought and decision-making – in other words, it makes it difficult for people to control their situations and achieve their objectives. This position may be called the dysfunctionalist. Of the metaphors treated above, culture as exchange-regulator and as compass have a clear functionalist bias. Culture as affect-regulator and as non-order are agnostic, culture as dramaturgical domination and world-closure sectional functionalist, and culture as blinders dysfunctionalist.

Another dimension is objectivism versus subjectivism, and it has two slightly different aspects: (1) social reality viewed as anchored in systems, structures, and other objective features as opposed to the minds and consciousness of actors in society and (2) social phenomena understood as objective, robust, real, and capable of being studied as natural phenomena (imitating the methodology of natural science) rather than as expressions of the subjectivity and consciousness of researchers (Burrell & Morgan, 1979). Oversimplifying, it might be suggested the exchange-regulator, compass, rites, and social-glue metaphors are objectivist and the blinders metaphor subjectivist, with the rest of the metaphors falling in between.

A third important dimension is cognition versus emotion. The exchange-regulator metaphor is highly cognitively oriented – relying on instrumentalism and self-interest as the only important motives – while the sacred-cow, affect-regulator, and blinders metaphors give priority to affect aspects of culture. The rest of the metaphors occupy a less clear-cut position.

A fourth dimension is free will versus determinism. To what extent can people control culture and to what extent are they controlled by it? Some authors, typically those with a strong managerial interest, adopt a dualistic position. The rites and blinders metaphors portray managers as (potentially) in control of culture while employees respond passively to their dictates. The world-closure and dramaturgical-domination metaphors point to differences between participants in asymmetrical power relations but recognize that subordinates have the chance of opposing power, and the social-glue metaphor (as Ray uses it) seems to agree. The compass and exchange-regulator metaphors represent a more traditional determinist position: the active engagement of participants is not visible, and 'variables' of other kinds explain outcomes.

One final dimension worth mentioning is pro-management versus anti-management. Here the rites metaphor (as used by Trice & Beyer) is extremely pro-management, the world-closure and dramaturgical-domination metaphors are radical-critical and anti-management, and the other relatively neutral.

All metaphors – including the culture metaphors mentioned here – are necessarily reductionist. The pro-management ones, for example, stress the positive effects of culture, the anti-management ones the ways in which culture, through manipulation by elite actors or through tradition and socialization, contributes to the fixing and freezing of the sociocultural order. Evaluation of organizational culture studies is therefore to a large extent a matter of discussing the benefits and drawbacks of different forms of reductionism: reductionism which aims at equipping managers with the means for increased effectiveness and reductionism which aims at highlighting how the open and negotiable character of the social world is obscured by various forms of domination.

Notes

1 The two views of metaphor are incommensurable in Kuhn's (1970) terms; their arguments cannot really be evaluated independently of their respective paradigmatic assumptions. Although various suggestions have been made for achieving partial understanding across paradigms through dialogue and debate, the communication difficulties of scholars involved in different 'language games' should not be under estimated (see Bernstein, 1983; Jackson & Willmott, 1987).

2 The distinction is not as clear as it might appear, however, because focusing on the implicit and not clearly recognized metaphors in research may mean that these appear new, thus functioning in a creative way. By signifying the implicit, new ideas may be encouraged.

3 According to the garbage-can model, decisions result from the random convergence of streams of problems, solutions, people, and situations.

4 Of course, the risk of reductionism is inherent in all perspectives/metaphors. The traditional reductionism associated with mechanistic and organismic metaphors is likely to be much more problematic than a strict utilization of the culture-as-metaphor view.

5 Many researchers of organizational culture in fact stress 'organization' more than 'culture', and for them organizational culture is as organized, systemic, and order-creating as 'organization' itself.

The culture–performance link

Although organizational culture research has produced some new insights about the long-neglected, subjective or 'soft' side of organizational life, many aspects of it that might be explored from a cultural perspective have not yet received much attention. Instead, emphasis has been placed primarily on the cultural and symbolic aspects that are relevant in an instrumental/pragmatic context. In this regard, Ouchi and Wilkins (1985: 462) note that 'the contemporary student of organizational culture often takes the organization not as a natural solution to deep and universal forces but rather as a rational instrument designed by top management to shape the behavior of the employees in purposive ways'. Accordingly, much research on corporate culture and organizational symbolism is dominated by a preoccupation with a limited set of meanings, symbols, values, and ideas presumed to be manageable and directly related to effectiveness and performance. It would of course be difficult to take everything into account in any one study, but it seems strange that the literature should generally disregard such values as bureaucratic-'meritocratic' hierarchy, unequal distribution of privileges and rewards, a mixture of individualism and conformity, male domination, emphasis on money, economic growth, advanced technology, exploitation of nature, and the equation of economic criteria with rationality. Instrumental reason dominates: quantifiable values and the optimization of means for the attainment of pre-given ends define rationality (Horkheimer & Adorno, 1947; Marcuse, 1964). The values to which organizational culture research pays attention are primarily connected with the means and operations employed to achieve goals.

The dominance of instrumental values

The more popular literature argues that 'good' or 'valuable' cultures – often equated with 'strong' cultures – are characterized by norms beneficial to the company, to customers, and to mankind and by 'good' performance in general:

27

> Good cultures are characterized by norms and values supportive of excellence, teamwork, profitability, honesty, a customer service orientation, pride in one's work, and commitment to the organization. Most of all, they are supportive of adaptability – the capacity to thrive over the long run despite new competition, new regulations, new technological developments, and the strains of growth. (Baker, 1980: 10)

In most cases the values and beliefs of interest are closely related to virtues, attitudes, and behaviour useful to the achievement of corporate goals as defined by management (e.g., Deal & Kennedy, 1982; Peters & Waterman, 1982; Trice & Beyer, 1985) and are therefore largely instrumental in character. In different companies they are 'norms supporting innovation', 'cost consciousness norms', and 'norms that support rapid growth' (Baker, 1980: 10–11). Wiener's (1988: 536) assertion that 'the wrong values make the culture a major liability' has already been mentioned. Similarly, Kilmann, Saxon, Serpa, *et al.* (1985: 4) argue that 'a culture has a positive impact on an organization when it points behavior in the right direction.... Alternatively, a culture has negative impact when it points behavior in the wrong direction.' According to Wilkins and Patterson (1985: 272), 'The ideal culture ... is characterized by a clear assumption of equity ... a clear sense of collective competence ... and an ability to continually apply the collective competence to new situations as well as to alter it when necessary' (see also Gagliardi, 1986). Kanter (1983) talks about 'cultures of pride', which are good, and 'cultures of inferiority', which any sane person will avoid. This type of functionalist, normative, and instrumentally biased conceptualization of culture is also found in Schein's (1985) influential exposition, in which culture is seen as a pattern of basic assumption that has 'proved' to be valid for a group coping with problems of external adaptation and internal integration. Basically, culture in this literature is instrumental in relation to the formal goals of an organization and to the management objectives or tasks associated with these goals (i.e., external and internal effectiveness). It is assumed to exist because it works. Of course, changed circumstances can make a culture dysfunctional – calling for planned, intentional change – but the approach assumes that culture is or can be 'good' for some worthwhile purpose. ('Good' and 'bad' are not, however, self-evident, especially when it comes to complex phenomena such as culture.)

The instrumental and normative bias is especially strong in the study of (cultural) change. According to Wilkins and Dyer (1987), almost all approaches begin by explicitly or implicitly asking the following questions. (1) What should organizational culture look like if it is to support the organization's strategy? (2) What does current organizational culture look like, and what are the gaps between this and the culture needed? (3) What plan of action should be followed to close the gaps? Consequently, studies of cultural change (often equated with purposive and manager-induced change) largely neglect those aspects of change which are not directly relevant from a strategic point of view (and therefore, probably, most aspects of change). Changes are viewed through managerial lenses, and the understanding of cultural change which emerges is, to say the least, selective, and may be misleading.

Without in any way suggesting that planned change or the role of management in change should be neglected, one can point to other interesting aspects of cultural change: organic change following from the historical development of the organization, gradual change in character over time, and the effects of cultural changes in the society at large, which according to Deetz (1985: 255) 'frequently have more impact on productivity, motivation, and morale than any managerial decision'. A better understanding of cultural change in organizations would call not only for instrumentally oriented projects but also for studies of unplanned change and change from points of view other than that of management.

One consequence of this functionalist/pragmatic approach is that culture tends to be reduced to those limited aspects of this complex phenomenon that are perceived to be directly related to organizational efficiency and competitive advantage (see, e.g., Barney, 1986, and most of the papers in Kilmann *et al.*, 1985). It may even be equated with certain behavioural norms viewed as 'an excellent vehicle for helping people understand and manage the cultural aspects of organizational life' (Allen, 1985: 334). The problem, of course, is that norms are not the best vehicle for understanding culture. Whereas norms tell people how to behave, culture has a much broader and more complex influence on thinking, feeling, and sense-making (Schneider, 1976). Again, Barney (1986) argues that to serve as a source of sustained competitive advantage culture must be 'valuable, rare, and imperfectly imitable'. If this statement is to make any sense at all, culture must be interpreted as highly normative, accessible to evaluation in terms of frequency (i.e., quantifiable), and capable of being copied at will. This banal conception deprives culture of the richness that is normally seen as its strength.

Another example of this trivialization of culture is the confusion of organizational culture with the firm's management ideology. As is pointed out by Westley and Jaeger (1985), in much discussion culture really stands for the somewhat simpler concept of ideology: a relatively restricted set of norms and values indicating important ideals and visions for a group (see also Alvesson, 1987).[1] It is sometimes held that the best way to investigate 'corporate culture' is through interviews with top managers, but the outcome of this approach tends to be a description of the espoused ideology of those managers. Organizational culture and managerial ideology are not the same.

Westley and Jaeger (1985: 15) suggest that cultural studies should be permitted to develop unrestricted by concerns for practicality: 'The more rigorously
(anthropologically) the term (culture) is applied, the more the concept of
organizational culture gains in theoretical interpretative power and the more it
loses in practicality. In the effort to overcome this contradiction the danger is
that theoretical rigour will be lost in the interest of practicality.' Even when the
conceptualization of culture is more rigorous – for example, when it is suggested
that culture can be influenced only to a limited extent and then only with
difficulty (e.g., Berg, 1985a; Martin & Siehl, 1983) – and when the focus is not
on the possibility of manipulation, there is often an implicit preoccupation with
questions relevant to managers, consultants, and others assumed to act with the
organizational cultures being examined with a view to improving the functioning
of the organizations. A bias towards the 'positive' functions of culture and its
close relation to issues such as harmony, consensus, clarity, and meaningfulness
is also implicit in many of these studies (see Martin & Meyerson, 1988).[2]
Symbols and cultural aspects are often seen as functional (or dysfunctional) for
the organization in terms of goal attainment, meeting the emotional-expressive
needs of members, reducing tension in communication, and so on. Instru-
mental/functional dimensions are often emphasized, for instance, in studies of
rites and ceremonies (e.g., Dandridge, 1986; Trice & Beyer, 1984). The typical
research focus is on social integration (Alvesson, 1987). Culture is understood as
(usually or potentially) useful, and those aspects of culture that are not easily or
directly seen as useful remain out of sight. The most common ideas guiding
organizational analysis draw upon such metaphors for culture as tool, need
satisfier, or regulator of social relations.

Before assuming that culture is functional or good for organizational or
managerial purposes, it makes sense to distinguish among its various functions
and to recognize that they may conflict. Critical reflection and learning may be a
good thing, consensus facilitating control and coordinated action another, and
reduction of anxiety a third, but not all these good things may be attainable at the
same time. Perhaps more important, contradictory interests – those of professions, divisions, classes, consumers, environmentalists, the state, owners, top
management, etc. – may produce different views on what is good, important, and
appropriate. Culture is a complex set of aspects some of which may be related to
organizational processes and outcomes while some point in other directions, and
most aspects are difficult to designate as clearly good or bad. To simplify these
relationships runs the risk of producing misleading pictures of cultural manifestations. Instead, 'our focus must become the tensions between the creative and
destructive possibilities of culture formation' (Jeffcutt, 1993).

Oversimplification does not necessarily serve narrow pragmatic interests.

Making things look clear-cut and simple may mislead. Practitioners might benefit much more from the pro-managerial and pragmatic organizational culture literature if it stopped focusing on how to manage and control culture and instead discussed other phenomena which managers might, with luck and skill, be able to manage and control – for example, workplace spirit and behavioural norms. Learning to 'think culturally' about organizational reality might inspire enlightened managerial action rather than unrealistic programmes for culture change.

Theoretical approaches to the culture–performance link

The contemporary literature on the relevance of organizational culture to corporate performance can be classified in terms of the degree to which instrumental values prevail.

In the most instrumentally oriented of these formulations, culture is conceived as a building block in organizational design – a subsystem, well-demarcated from other parts of the organization, which includes norms, values, beliefs, and behavioural styles of employees. Even though it may be difficult to master, it is in principle no different from other parts of the organization in terms of management and control. The term 'cultural engineering' captures the spirit of this position (Alvesson & Berg, 1992), which is sometimes called the 'corporate-culture school'. Proponents of this view of culture include Cummings (1984), Deal and Kennedy (1982), and Kilmann (1985) among others.

Kilmann (1985: 354) recognizes that there is considerable disagreement about what culture is but concludes that 'it is still important to consider what makes a culture good or bad, adaptive or dysfunctional'. He describes culture almost as a physical force: 'Culture provides meaning, direction, and mobilization – it is the social energy that moves the corporation into allocation. . . . the energy that flows from shared commitments among group members' (p. 352) and 'the force controlling behaviour at every level in the organization' (p. 358). He believes that every firm has a distinctive culture that can develop and change quickly and must be managed and controlled: 'If left alone, a culture eventually becomes dysfunctional' (p. 354).

The crucial dimension of culture, according to Kilmann, is norms; it is here that culture is 'most easily controlled'. More precisely, it is the norms that guide the behaviour and attitudes of the people in the company that are of greatest interest and significance, because they have a powerful effect on the requirements for its success – quality, efficiency, product reliability, customer service, innovation, hard work, loyalty, etc. This is the core of most (American) texts on corporate culture (e.g., Deal & Kennedy, 1982; Peters & Waterman, 1982;

Sathe, 1985; Wiener, 1988). There are, of course, many difficulties with this model.

For example, Sathe (1985: 236) argues that 'the strength of a culture influences the intensity of behavior', and the 'strength' of a culture is determined by 'how many important shared assumptions there are', how widely they are shared, and how clearly they are ranked. A 'strong' culture is thus characterized by homogeneity, simplicity, and clearly ordered assumptions. In a 'complex' culture – by definition any culture – assumptions will probably be very difficult to identify and rank, and it can even be argued that such a measurement approach distorts the phenomena it is supposed to study. As Fitzgerald (1988: 9–10) has put it:

> values do not exist as isolated, independent, or incremental entities. Beliefs and assumptions, tastes and inclinations, hopes and purposes, values and principles are not modular packages stored on warehouse shelves, waiting for inventory. They have no separate existence, as do spark plugs in an engine; they cannot be examined one at a time and replaced when burned out.... They have their own inner dynamic: Patriotism, dignity, order, progress, equality, security – each implies other values, as well as their opposites. Patriotism implies homeland, duty, and honor, but also takes its strength from its contrast to disloyalty; dignity requires the possibility of humiliation and shame. Values form a knotted (if unsymmetrical) net that we cannot unravel without altering their reciprocity, harmonies, and synergy.

Moreover, to suggest that cultures can be measured on the single dimension of 'strength' is an oversimplification; a more accurate picture would suggest a shifting constellation of meanings more or less connected to various interests (Young, 1989: 190). Sathe's statement is doubly in error when it comes to the 'quantification' of social reality. Apart from the impossibility of operationalizing cultural 'strength', it (absurdly) suggests that more culture results in more behaviour. Culture may instead be associated, for example, with extreme heterogeneity of behaviour or inactivity. A 'strong' or distinct culture may mean either conformism or pluralism, action orientation or introspection and reflection.

Another problem with this approach is the tendency to view norms and values as capable of being abstracted from other things in an organization. Kilmann, Sathe, Deal, and Kennedy, and other 'corporate-culture' writers propose that, other things being equal, a company-wide set of norms and values can be affected by the same external forces, and be the cause of behaviour and performance. This conceptualization is problematic because, among other things, work norms are probably closely tied to a variety of circumstances in the workplace rather than being organization-wide. The kind of job and organization, the reward structure, and the employee's age, gender, qualifications, and interests are probably more significant in determining these norms. Hofstede *et al.* (1990), for example, found age, educational level, and hierarchical position to predict work values. To try to isolate norms and values shared throughout the organization (or any other large unit) as a separate causal factor in work performance is probably a hopeless task. This is not to say that norms do not matter. Rather, to a large degree they are probably associated with different groups to different degrees and have different content. For example, on the shopfloor, output restriction is reported to be a common norm, and it is probably seldom shared by management.

It would in fact be odd if CEOs, typists, factory workers, salesmen, engineers, and product designers shared norms and acted upon them in similar ways. Division of labour is a cornerstone of the modern corporation, and norms that opposed rather than reflected diversity would not necessarily make it more efficient. It might be – and sometimes is – argued that 'corporate culture' counteracts the disintegration fostered by the vertical and horizontal differentiation of modern organizations. But to the extent that this is the case, probably less is achieved through organization-wide norms which directly affect behaviour in a homogeneous way than through shared feelings of identification and community. Therefore it is important to distinguish between common culture as a source of feelings of togetherness, belonging, and mutual understanding and culture as something which directly affects behaviour through norms. The conclusion suggested here is that the values and norms which comprise 'corporate culture' have very limited direct impact on organizational effectiveness in terms of work behaviour and willingness to work.

A second category of approaches linking organizational culture with performance assumes that the leadership of an organization exercises more or less far-reaching influence on the way in which employees perceive and understand their tasks and on the workplace by creating and maintaining metaphors and myths. One result of this type of influence, from management's point of view, might be the sharing of a 'favourable' definition of organizational reality and work by the whole collective (the organization, a department, a division, or some other subgroup). Proponents of this approach, known as symbolic management, include Berg (1986), Pfeffer (1981), and Smircich and Morgan (1982).

Pfeffer (1981) distinguishes between internal, management control and external, environmental control (such as market conditions and other forms of external resource dependencies (cf. Pfeffer & Salancik, 1978)) and between substantive outcomes (actions and activities which lead to tangible, measurable results and have physical referents, such as budgets, salary allocations, sales, and profits) and symbolic outcomes (attitudes, sentiments, values, and perceptions). He suggests that while constraints beyond managerial control basically determine the substantive outcomes, management does have far-reaching influence on employees' attitudes to social reality. The symbolic outcomes of managerial action increase the probability of the development of a common set of understandings about organizational affairs among members.[3] Managerial action – and 'culture' (although Pfeffer does not explicitly use this concept) – involves the development of consensus around the definition of workplace activity (p. 21).[4] Pfeffer is careful to point out that this consensus is not necessarily about values and goals but rather about means and technology, and here he sharply differs from most other writers on organizational culture (cf., e.g., Kilmann above).

Pfeffer considers any linkage between symbolic and substantive outcomes weak and indirect. Perception and understanding are less a cause than a consequence of behaviour and outcomes. The most important behaviour patterns are basically determined by external constraints. The cultural dimension is more a stabilizing force: 'Shared understandings are likely to emerge to rationalize the patterns of behavior that develop, and in the absence of such rationalization and meaning creation, the structured patterns of behavior are likely to be less stable and persistent' (p. 14). Some possible consequences of symbolic action include mobilization/motivation, satisfaction of demands, implementation of change, and, most important, attitudes and feelings of satisfaction. Clever symbolic action may partly replace 'substance' in an ambiguous situation and thus increase the satisfaction felt by a group without any 'real', substantive change: 'Symbolic actions may serve to mollify groups that are dissatisfied with the organization, thereby ensuring their continued support of the organization and the lessening of opposition and conflict' (p. 35). Symbolic action may also produce commitment and identification with the company. Pfeffer is more careful, then, than most writers on 'corporate culture' about postulating causal relations between culture and corporate performance, instead stressing the avoidance of problems which might negatively affect organizational performance such as conflict, resistance, widespread frustration, high turnover, and absenteeism.

With regard to the effects he talks about as a product of (managerial) action, whereas it is true that social processes intervene in the perception of as well as the creation of social reality, these social processes are themselves governed by (socially constructed and material) 'reality'. In other words, the substantive aspects of a job situation have symbolic consequences. Although Pfeffer refers to Berger and Luckmann's (1966) concept of the social construction of social reality, he overlooks the historical dimension of this process. Our world view and patterns of social perception are historically anchored, and this may make perceptions, attitudes, and sentiments difficult to alter. Furthermore, he tends to underestimate the multiplicity of sources of socially governed perceptions and understandings of organizational affairs. Van Maanen and Barley (1984; 1985) suggest that the great variety of professions and occupations in most complex organizations may create social conflict and competitive definitions of reality and that this tendency may be reinforced by new technology. This means that consensus over technology may be less prevalent than Pfeffer seems to indicate. Pfeffer refers to organizations as paradigms. A more appropriate albeit less elegant metaphor might be the pre-paradigmatic field of knowledge, in which members of several groups share perceptions and understandings of technologies, knowledge, and problem-solving among themselves, but intergroup relations do not always facilitate cooperation and harmony. The metaphor of organizations as pre-paradigms has the advantage of indicating the lack of maturity and absence of broad agreement that characterize many organizations, in contrast to the hegemony of ideas and homogenization of social knowledge that the Kuhnian paradigm concept implies. This is not to deny that managerial action may affect how social reality is perceived in a way that leads to shared beliefs and understandings (or at least reduced diversity in these regards). The outcome of this may be stabilizing, serving to reduce conflict about technologies and negative evaluations of ambiguous situations and conditions. At the same time, the extent to which this action can produce an organizational paradigm remains an open question.

A third category of studies focusing on organizational culture and performance employs culture as a diagnostic instrument and a guide for action. It stresses the deep values and basic assumptions of organizations – unconscious or half-conscious beliefs and ideals about objectives, relationships to the external world, and the internal relations that underlie behavioural norms, action rules and priorities, and other 'artifacts'. Culture is viewed as resistant to attempts at understanding or change and only occasionally manageable. This approach is not much concerned about pragmatic issues, but it does attempt to be of practical relevance by informing managers of what may be difficult or impossible to accomplish because of cultural restrictions and providing ideas for constructive action in the light of culture. Researchers adopting this position are e.g. Louis (1985), Lundberg (1985), Martin and Siehl (1983), and Schein (1985).

The focus here is not on the effects of managerial action but rather on the effects of local cultures, which through tradition are anchored in the organizational collective and exercise influence without the direct or immediate involvement of particular key actors. For Schein (1985: 9) culture is 'a pattern of basic assumptions – invented, discovered, or developed by a given group as it learns to cope with its problems of external adaptation and internal integration – that has worked well enough to be considered valid and therefore, to be taught to new members as the correct way to perceive, think, and feel in relation to those problems'. Indeed, members will find behaviour based on any other premise inconceivable. Artifacts are the visible and audible patterns of culture, existing on a surface level, and values, on the intermediary level, concern what 'ought' to be done and are more or less understood and consciously grasped by the organizational community.

Schein suggests that cultural phenomena have far-reaching effects on organizational effectiveness and individual satisfaction. As examples he points to the effects of culture on strategy, mergers, acquisitions, and diversifications, the integration of new technologies, intergroup conflicts within the organization, the effectiveness of communication, socialization, and the level of productivity. The linkages he suggests seem intuitively correct, but a careful reading raises doubts about the causal relationship presumed.

One example concerns a company that had become successful by marketing a very complex product to sophisticated consumers:

> When the company later developed a smaller, simpler, less expensive version of this product, which could be sold to less sophisticated customers, its product designers and its marketing and sales divisions could not deal with the new customer type. The sales and marketing people could not imagine what the concerns of the new, less knowledgeable customer might be, and the product designers continued to be convinced that they could judge product attractiveness themselves. Neither group was motivated to understand the new customer type because, unconsciously, they tended to look down on such customers. (Schein, 1985: 32)

He suggests that this problem was not merely one of inadequate training but 'cultural' in nature: 'the perceptions and resulting behaviour patterns were built on deeply held, long-standing assumptions that were taken-for-granted because they had led to prior success'. The 'deeply held, long-standing assumption' in question is presumably that the company would manufacture and sell a complex product to sophisticated customers. Apparently, much of the organization did not any longer share this assumption, and in fact a simpler version of the product for a less sophisticated consumer group was developed, produced, and marketed. Those who took the former situation for granted might resist change, have a low opinion of it, or be less skilled in dealing with a certain type of customer, but this does not really touch upon the deep level which Schein sees as the crucial one.

From Schein's description, it seems that the company was unable to understand and judge the concerns and tastes of its customers; it may be speculative to bring basic assumptions in to the discussion. Working for some time with a particular object will produce competence, not only in the strictly technical sense but also in a somewhat wider social or cultural one, in line with the demands of that object. Dealing with a new customer group will require the development of new capacities for understanding their concerns and tastes. An inability to understand and communicate with new customers may be the result of a lack of the required social and cultural skills. Negative attitudes and traditional values may of course be of some significance here, but a simpler explanation than Schein's would appear to be sufficient.

Another of Schein's examples concerns the acquisition of a franchised business:

> The lack of understanding of the cultural risks of buying a franchised business was brought out even more clearly in another case, where a very stuffy, traditional, moralistic company whose management prided itself on its high ethical standards bought a chain of fast-food restaurants that were locally franchised around the country. The company's managers discovered, much to their chagrin, that one of the biggest of these restaurants in a nearby state had become the local brothel. The activities of the town were so well integrated around this restaurant that the alternative of closing it down posed the risk of drawing precisely the kind of attention this company wanted at all costs to avoid. The managers asked themselves, *after the fact*, 'Should we have known what our acquisition involved on this more subtle level? Should we have understood our own value system better, to ensure compatibility?' (Schein, 1985: 34–5)

Here the problem seems to be lack of knowledge on a very specific point – what the company was buying – rather than lack of understanding of the company's own value system. Most ordinary, 'respectable' corporations, whatever their organizational culture, would probably wish to avoid becoming owners of brothels.

A third example concerns a large packaged foods company which had purchased a chain of fast-food restaurants. The new people brought in to manage them did not understand the technology of the fast-food business, and problems of gaining the right 'feel' for its new acquisition ultimately forced the company to sell it. Here too it is difficult to see the specific importance of culture in Schein's sense (basic assumptions).

A very different type of cultural effect, according to Schein, concerns productivity:

> Work groups form strong cultures, and often such subcultures develop the assumption that work should be limited not by what one is able to do but what is appropriate to do – 'a fair day's work for a fair day's pay'. Sometimes, when the organization is seen to be in trouble or when workers link their own self-interest to that of the company, the norm is towards high productivity, but typically the norm 'restricts' output. (Schein, 1985: 43)

In this case, too, his concept of culture hardly explains the outcome (a particular level of productivity); it is a long step from basic assumptions and deep values to the behavioural norms of performance. As Schein indicates, these norms vary with the circumstances, such as the economic situation and the risk of layoffs. In one or two cases (e.g., intergroup conflicts), his concept of culture appears to fit, but more often it is difficult to see a clear link between culture as he conceives it and organizational effectiveness.

In an overview article on the investigation of workplace cultures, Louis characterizes culture as

> a set of understandings or *meanings shared* by a group of people. The meanings are largely *tacit* among members, are clearly *relevant* to the particular group, and are *distinctive* to the group. Meanings are *passed on* to new group members.... [culture's content is] the totality of socially transmitted behavior patterns, a style of social and artistic expression, a set of common understandings. (1985: 74)

She cites four examples of the effects of workplace culture: increase in the safety and meaningfulness of work through team-oriented work in coal mines (Trist & Bamforth, 1951), increase in workers' commitment to and identification with a group and organization, elimination of the need for structural controls to induce desired attitudes and behaviour, and facilitation of the socialization of new members.

To some extent, the critical comments made about Kilmann's approach to culture as a behaviour-regulator are valid here, but beyond this, given Louis's definition of culture, it is difficult to see how culture and the outcomes of culture can be separated. If culture *is* meanings and socially transmitted behaviour patterns, how can it then *induce* attitudes and behaviours and replace structural controls? Again, the teamwork in the coal mines is not necessarily an *effect* of the culture there; the work situation and its teamwork orientation may produce a certain culture. Even better, one might say that the workplace culture cannot be separated from the way the job is performed and therefore no causal relationship can be established. Workplace culture *is* a way (a set of aspects) of doing a job – the shared meanings and understandings surrounding a certain kind of work as a social practice.

The same holds for the statement that 'the socialization of new members is facilitated by work group cultures' (p. 85); without culture, socialization is impossible, and without socialization there would be no one to 'carry' culture. Furthermore, if there were no specific work-group culture, there would be no need for socialization: people would fit in anyway as a result of a shared broader culture associated with nation, class, profession, etc. (Similar remarks can be made against Schein (1985) who also argues that culture and socialization are related.)

That workplace cultures affect workers' commitment to and identification with groups and organizations also tends towards tautology. Culture includes a certain similarity among the people involved, and identification and similarity go together. At the same time, a culture need not include value consensus, community feelings, etc., but may be based on individualism, self-interest, competition, and careerism, and here it will not involve commitment and identification. Like most organizational culture researchers talking about outcomes of culture, Louis seems to have 'positive' cultures in mind.

I do not disagree with Louis that workplace culture is important to an understanding of workers' commitment and identification with the workplace. Improved work safety in the coal mine and attention to the welfare of the families of work group members could also be interpreted as outcomes of workplace culture. The general impression of Louis' account of 'outcomes of workplace culture', however, is that it is often difficult to separate clearly what is culture and what is its outcomes; Louis' definition of culture seems to include much of what is generally presented as outcomes of culture.

Empirical studies

The discussion so far has been dealing primarily with conceptual problems and difficulties in theoretical reasoning. These aspects are naturally also crucial to empirical studies, so let us now turn to empirical investigations of culture-performance relationships.

Empirical studies of organizational culture have mainly examined the so-called strong-culture thesis. It has often been assumed that commitment of an organization's employees and managers to the same set of values, beliefs, and norms will have positive results – that the 'strength' of 'corporate culture' is directly correlated with the level of profits in a company (e.g., Denison, 1984). Researchers adopting this hypothesis tend to place new kinds of human relations (involving employees in decision-making, allowing them some discretion, developing holistic relations, etc.) at the core of organizational culture (e.g., Peters & Waterman, 1982; Ouchi, 1981). Another common hypothesis about the link between culture and performance in empirical studies suggests the reverse relationship: that high performance leads to the creation of a 'strong' corporate culture (cultural homogeneity). Still another idea draws upon contingency thinking to suggest that under certain conditions a particular type of culture is appropriate, even necessary, and contributes to efficiency. Wilkins and Ouchi (1983), for example, consider culture an important regulatory mechanism in organizational settings too complex and ambiguous to be controlled by traditional means (bureaucracy and the market).

Siehl and Martin (1990), having reviewed the few empirical studies in this area and conducted a study of their own, conclude that none of these three hypotheses on the culture–performance link has received much empirical support, and Calori and Sarnin (1991) confirm this conclusion. Siehl and Martin find important methodological deficiencies in all these studies and suggest that the culture concept cannot be linked so closely to corporate results.

Of course, failure to establish an empirical link does not mean that no such link exists. Not only is culture difficult to capture but so is performance (Sköldberg, 1990). It is common sense that something that we can call 'corporate culture' will have an impact on many types of actions in organizations and consequently also on corporate financial results. Any such influence may, however, be lost among all the factors and interaction patterns that have something to do with these results. Bhaskar's distinction between 'the domain of the empirical', experiences created by direct and indirect observation, and 'the domain of the real', events which take place whether or not we observe them, is useful here (Outhwaite, 1983). The actual is distinct from the real partly because not everything is observed and partly because not everything is observable. This view strongly warns against an empiricist approach. In the absence of opportunities to 'observe' culture and its role, we can of course speculate about it. As we have seen, however, such speculation is also problematic.

Instead of giving up the idea of finding clear-cut empirical answers to the question of 'corporate culture's' effect on performance, some researchers have argued that a more refined approach which takes into account the complexity of culture should guide empirical studies. Saffold (1988: 546), for example, argues that it is reasonable to expect that 'a phenomenon as pervasive as organizational culture affects organizational performance' but current models oversimplify the relationship. He points to five important shortcomings of empirical studies: (1) 'Strong-culture' studies tend to emphasize a single, unitary organizational culture even though multiple subcultures rather than unitary cultures seem to be the rule. (2) Measures of the 'strength' of culture are ambiguous partly because in the study of culture 'meanings are central, not frequencies' (Van Maanen & Barley, 1984: 307). (3) There is a preference for broad-brush cultural profiles, focusing on very general values and norms, which fail to do justice to the complexity of culture. (4) There is insufficient attention to the variety of possible culture–performance links. A particular cultural feature may affect different performance-related organizational processes in different directions. Development of shared meanings may, for example, have a positive effect on organizational control but at the same time create conformism and reduce the organization's capacity to learn and change. (5) There are many methodological problems in existing studies, ranging from overreliance on top management views to the absence of control groups.

Saffold goes on to suggest an enriched framework which involves the 'use of appropriate measures of culture's impact', the use of contextual rather than modal analysis (i.e., avoidance of static and abstract categorizations), and attention to multiple interactions. This framework involves (1) measures of cultural dispersion, the degree to which cultural characteristics are dispersed throughout an organization (sociologically, psychologically, historically, and artifactually); (2) measures of cultural potency (the power of the culture itself to influence behaviour); (3) studies of 'how specific culturally conditioned processes contribute to outcomes', and (4) the recognition of multiple, mutually causal interactions. Hardly surprisingly, he notes that 'if it all sounds complex, it is – unavoidably so', but believes that his framework 'reflects the true richness of culture–performance relationships'. In this observation he is probably correct.

Saffold's 'three correctives' will probably discourage researchers from attempting the task of studying culture-performance relationships. Siehl and Martin (1990) suggest that there are more worthwhile projects, and it is surprising that Saffold does not seem to draw this conclusion himself. His hope of advancing the study of the culture–performance link reflects the dominance of pragmatic/instrumental preoccupations in organizational culture studies. 'Corporate culture' has emerged as a key to corporate success, and doubts whether clear-cut empirical relations between the complex and elusive category of culture and performance criteria can be established have apparently been subordinated to this idea.

The problems of culture as cause

One problem with the culture concept in organizational studies with pragmatic/ instrumental purposes is giving it a restricted and precise meaning. A list of current definitions of 'culture' leaves hardly any of what is thought, felt, intended, or done in organizations outside it: observed behavioural regularities, or 'the way we do things', in a particular corporation (e.g., Deal & Kennedy, 1982); a set of behavioural norms characterizing a company (e.g., Kilmann, 1985); 'a cognitive frame of reference and a pattern of behavior transmitted to members of a group from the previous generation of the group' (Beres & Porterwood, cited by Lundberg, 1985: 171; cf. Louis, 1985); 'shared social knowledge' (Wilkins & Ouchi, 1983); 'what people believe about what works and what does not' (Wilkins & Patterson, 1985: 267); 'the set of important assumptions (often unstated) that members of a community hold in common' (Sathe, 1985: 235); 'a shared system of values, norms, and symbols' (Louis, 1981: 249); 'the organization's expressive and affective dimensions in a system of shared and meaningful symbols' (Allaire & Firsirotu, 1984: 107); 'the shared philosophies, ideologies, values, assumptions, beliefs, expectations, attitudes and norms that knit a community together' (Kilmann *et al.*, 1985: 5). Given all that appears to be contained in the concept of culture, it is bound to appear to be relevant to various dimensions of organizational effectiveness as well as most other aspects of organizations. The popularity of 'corporate culture' as a tool for management is understandable.

The general conclusion which can be drawn from these investigations of the link between organizational culture and performance is that the idea of culture very often promises more than it delivers. I am not saying that there is no connection between culture (however defined) and performance; on a general level there certainly is. I agree with Whipp *et al.* (1989: 582) that 'elements of culture ... may supply vital links between the rational aspects of policy and the subjective, less tangible features of employees' behaviour exactly because of the way values pervade an enterprise'. Propositions of how precisely defined concepts of culture bring about distinct outcomes, however, often seem problematic. Either the causal link is speculative and uncertain or it is impossible to separate culture from outcome. Of the four approaches treated in some depth above (Kilmann, Pfeffer, Schein, and Louis), only Pfeffer's rather cautious formulation of the possible effects of symbolic action on attitudes and other 'non-substantive' aspects of organizations seems well founded, and even he seems to exaggerate the effects of symbolic management at the expense of 'material' factors, the inertia of socially constructed reality, and the multiplicity of 'paradigmatic sources' of organizations. The difficulty in separating 'culture' from 'non-culture' is repeatedly referred to by authors speculating about the implications of culture for organizational performance and other outcomes. In addition to the examples provided above, Gagliardi (1986: 124) claims that 'a common culture strengthens cohesion, improves the ability to communicate, allowing that the spirit, rather than the letter, of the organization's rules are observed'. It is hard to imagine that cohesion, ability to communicate, and a spirit of organizational rules would be possible without a common culture. These presumed outcomes exist to a greater or lesser extent in most definitions of culture (including Gagliardi's). As we have seen, there is a possibility that a culture might include anti-communal, individualistic and/or bureaucratic values which could produce outcomes other than those suggested by Gagliardi, but this possibility is not included in his view of culture as inherently 'good'. Thus this kind of statement appears either as tautological/trivial or in many cases – if the culture concept is stripped of a strong functionalistic bias and the possibility of anti-communal or bureaucratic values and ideals is acknowledged – as unfounded.[5] More generally, Pennings and Gresov (1986: 323) also refer to the difficulty of isolating values and norms and estimating their causal importance: 'the deterministic weight to be assigned to cultural factors is highly problematic. In assessing, for instance, the extent to which values determine behaviour, the best evidence of what values exist often lies in norms. But the existence of a norm is usually evidenced by regularities of behaviour and hence the whole explanation becomes tautological.'

Beyond the technical cognitive interest

An extreme response to all this might be that we should stop studying organizational culture. For the positivist and the pragmatist it may well be a dead end. There are, however, good reasons for studying culture from other perspectives and for other purposes. Instead of treating culture as a variable as most culture–performance approaches tend to do, it is possible to avoid the difficulty of attempting to distinguish between 'culture' and 'non-culture' or between culture and outcome and to establish causal relationships between culture and other variables by treating culture as a root metaphor. Culture in this sense can, of course, hardly be managed, controlled, or intentionally changed, and because culture as a 'whole' is more a perspective than an object one will tend to study the cultural dimensions of more restricted objects.

Whereas most of the studies that try to establish links between culture and performance proceed from what Habermas (1972) has called a technical cognitive interest – which aims at developing knowledge of cause-and-effect relations through which control over nature (and social life) can be achieved – the approach to culture that I am suggesting here proceeds from other cognitive interests that Habermas calls practical-hermeneutic and emancipatory. Practical-hermeneutic interest aims at achieving understanding about human existence – the creation of meaning and communication in order to produce knowledge about man as a cultural being, without any particular concern for the utility of that knowledge. Emancipatory interest aims at liberating humans from external and internal repressive forces which prevent them from acting upon their free choices (for applications of this three-term framework to organizational culture studies, see Knights & Willmott, 1987; Stablein & Nord, 1985).

Culture and symbolism research guided by practical-hermeneutic interest does not concern itself with what culture might accomplish or how this accomplishment might be improved but concentrates on the creation of inter-subjective meaning. 'Questions of interpretation and description take precedence over questions of function and causal explanations' (Sypher, Applegate, & Sypher, 1985: 17). A common aim is to understand 'how to achieve common interpretations of situations so that coordinated action is possible' (Smircich, 1983a: 351). Practical-hermeneutic interest seems to underlie much of the organizational communication literature (e.g., Putnam & Pacanowsky, 1983; Sypher *et al.*, 1985) but also has some place in more general organizational culture research.

The relatively few studies proceeding from emancipatory interest assume one of two forms in their efforts to 'unlock' a closed world view created by the unconscious or by pure habit and conservatism, by tradition, socialization, influence, or manipulation on the part of powerful actors such as top managers. One is a critique of ideologies and sociocultural processes in organizations in which asymmetrical power relations make their mark on people's consciousness. The use of the idea of 'corporate culture' may here appear as a way in which management instils favourable definitions of reality in the minds of employees, and domination through symbolism becomes the target (e.g., Alvesson, 1991; Knights & Willmott, 1987; Rosen, 1985; Willmott, 1993). The other emancipatory project aims at illuminating basic values and understandings – the cultural elements which tend to be taken for granted in organizations – with a view to counteracting ethnocentrism. Whereas it is sceptical of the values typically advocated by management, its scope is broader.[6]

Notes

1 For a more critical and complex view of ideology, see, e.g., Mumby (1988).
2 Jeffcutt (1993) describes the dominant orientation as follows: 'the organisation culture and symbolism literature is distinguished by heroic quests for closure, being dominated by authors adopting representational styles that privilege epic and romantic narratives over tragic and ironic forms. These representational strategies expose an overriding search for unity and harmony that suppresses division and disharmony.'
3 As many authors emphasize, all phenomena are symbolic in the sense that they must be put into a cultural framework in order to be understood (Sköldberg, 1990, Tompkins, 1987). Tangible things such as products and money are therefore also symbolic. In order to separate symbols with strong physical referents from other ('pure') symbols, Sköldberg (1990) talks about the latter as 'meta-symbolic'. Meta-symbolism refers to other more tangible forms of symbolism: a story or myth might symbolize certain social relations, which in themselves are symbolic. In order to separate the two forms of symbols (à la Pfeffer), as well as to remind ourselves that even 'substantive' phenomena are symbolic, we could refer to these as 'substantive-symbolic' as opposed to 'meta-symbolic'. A distinction such as Pfeffer makes between the substantive versus the symbolic could then be read as the substantive-symbolic versus the meta-symbolic. However, in our present context we have no need to call attention to the symbolic nature of substantive phenomena. The recognition of the basically symbolic character of management action makes Pfeffer's position different from that of a variable approach, and he relies rather heavily on culture as an organizing metaphor, but without using it as a root metaphor, as the dualism of his approach makes clear.
4 Pfeffer uses the metaphor 'paradigm' in referring to the overall patterns of an organization in these regards, but it is not any of the 'paradigms' of Kuhn (1970). Kuhn's metaphors for 'paradigm' are world view, community, and key exemplar (see

Masterman, 1970); in using various metaphors he is probably not atypical of scholars working with complex concepts and frameworks.

5 A related problem for many writers on organizational culture arises from the attempt to regard culture in organizations as something distinct from and extraneous to bureaucratization and the formal/structural controls. This is illustrated to some extent by the above quotation from Gagliardi, in which culture is perceived as reducing the impact of bureaucracy (rules). Wilkins and Ouchi (1983), for example, see bureaucracy and culture as alternative organizational forms, but the formalization of tasks, hierarchical structure, and working by the book are 'culture' just as much as anything else. Bureaucracy in a rational Weberian sense could be seen as a typical cultural phenomenon of modern organizations. Bureaucracy is certainly not devoid of symbols, values, and meanings. Many writers on organizational culture, guided by a technical interest, do not observe this possibility in their preoccupation with narrowing down culture to become a management tool. Naturally it is possible to distinguish between forms of control aimed at the cultural level (meanings, ideas) and others directed at behaviour (by way of supervision or rules), and these last can be treated in a 'non-cultural' way (using metaphors for organization other than cultural ones). Such a distinction is more appropriate than the view that distinguishes between culture and bureaucracy, for it indicates the intentions behind control rather than generally indicating how rules function. In this last case it would probably be more useful to pay serious attention to the cultural level – the meanings, understandings, beliefs, and symbolism developed around rules and obedience to rules.

6 According to proponents of post-modernism, the idea of emancipation through enlightened, critical reason reflects a typical Western view on the human subject. It is therefore wise to acknowledge that research aimed at critical enlightenment also has elements of parochialism.

THREE

An emancipatory approach to organizational culture: counteracting parochialism

One product of the pragmatic perspective that dominates organizational culture research is a tendency for scholars to become trapped by the unquestioned assumptions of Western managerial culture, without being able to investigate these critically for themselves. Cultural blindness and narrow-mindedness are not necessarily exclusive to the pragmatic, functionalist approach; they also characterize non-pragmatic research, i.e. interpretative research and possibly even studies of emancipatory intent. This chapter concentrates mainly on the pragmatic research, but mention will also be made of interpretative studies. Much of the criticism presented here applies to large sections of the field as a whole, which has not succeeded in setting Western organizational life in a broader, anthropological perspective, thus enabling us to see familiar issues in a new light and consequently to reconsider our frameworks and taken for granted assumptions.

Western managerial culture is often taken for granted

The narrow view of organizational culture described in the previous chapter has come about partly because of the close association between researchers and management culture that is more or less universal at the higher levels of business in the Western world and, to a considerable extent, in industrialized countries in general. Most of the basic values, orientations, and assumptions of Western culture – progress, efficiency, rationalization, productivity, advanced technology, exploitation of nature, control, hierarchy, and affluent consumption, among others – are shared by management researchers writing about organizational culture. Perhaps because of this, these values generally go unexamined. Organization theorists, especially in the United States, tend to subordinate their intellectual understanding to the interests of the dominant elites (Alvesson, 1987; Laurent, 1978). This is probably sometimes a conscious choice but often to some extent an effect of the confusion of the managerial interest with

46

'neutrality' and the general interest: 'Most organizational research implicitly adopts this managerial bias, not simply because it is more interested in the managerial perspective, but largely because the so-called value-neutrality of scientific research is easily co-opted by dominant managerial interests. Research questions thus get framed from a managerial perspective, and findings are couched in managerial language' (Mumby, 1988: 2).

The tendency to view culture primarily through metaphors such as that of a resource or an instrument means that attention is concentrated on the manageable dimensions while the deeper layers of culture and the cultural context of organizations and managerial action are taken for granted. By 'deeper' here I mean aspects of a collective consciousness of which people are not fully aware but which they experience as the natural order or as pure rationality. Bourdieu (1979) addresses this basic level in terms of 'schemas' and 'habitus' acquired through socialization, and, as we have seen, Schein (1985) speaks of basic assumptions on a pre-conscious level. Researchers tend to view the cultural phenomena they encounter as natural, part of the world order, rather than as specific to national or late-capitalist/post-industrial society and business culture. Some discussion of this parochialism in management and organization research in general can be found in Boyacigillar and Adler (1991). Organizational culture research does not, on the whole perform better on this dimension than organization theory in general. This is ironic, since the proponents of the 'corporate-culture' approach have sometimes claimed that 'the essence of culture lies in the unstated premises or ethos that are taken for granted and so are largely implicit' (Trice & Beyer, 1984: 664). Gregory (1983: 359), an anthropologist, is exceptional in remarking that the literature concerned with organizational culture often says 'more about the culture of the researchers than the researched'. This kind of research problem is in fact more generally recognized by anthropologists (Marcus & Fischer, 1986); some even warn against the study of one's own society. Leach (1982: 124), for example, writes that 'fieldwork in a cultural context of which you already have intimate first-hand experience seems to be much more difficult than fieldwork which is approached from the naive viewpoint of a total stranger. When anthropologists study facets of their own society their vision seems to become distorted by prejudices which derive from private rather than public experience.' An interesting illustration of this cultural blindness is the fact that few organizational culture researchers have observed that the preoccupation with 'managing', 'organizing', and making like as 'efficient' as possible is a key feature of Western culture and of business organizations in particular. Smircich (1985: 56), however, has speculated on the way in which anthropologists a thousand years from now may characterize our societal and organizational culture: 'These people were crazy for organization. They

valued discipline, order, regulation, and obedience much more than indepen-
dence, expressiveness, and creativity. They were always looking for efficiency.
They wanted to control everything. They had a fetish for "managing", They
managed stress, time, relationships, emotions, but mostly they managed their
careers.'

The reduction of the culture concept to fit instrumental concerns and the
tendency to take Western managerial culture for granted may be viewed as quite
independent of each other. Normative research does not necessarily exclude
creative efforts in which cultural phenomena previously taken for granted are
investigated in a novel light (despite certain weaknesses, the work of Peters and
Waterman [1982], for example, does manage to shed new light on conventional
wisdom); and a broader approach that addresses not only minor, company-
related cultural variations but also the common assumptions, values, and
symbolism of Western business and working life is of course no guarantee of the
achievement of new insights. However, the two problems do overlap to some
extent. The instrumentally guided conceptualization of culture is a reduction of
its potential richness. From another angle, the inability to recognize and
interpret the basic cultural patterns of organizations in late-capitalist/post-
industrial society leads to a focus on what is specific to a certain company, for
example, its particular strategy or management style, and from this focus may
spring an emphasis on the instrumental elements of corporate culture specific to
that company. Our ability to think culturally is thus threatened from two
directions.

The two problems are also related in a specific and significant way. Because
the ideal of instrumental rationality is (though often imperfectly realized) a key
feature of Western society and, in particular, of business life (Alvesson, 1987;
Deetz & Kersten, 1983; Horkheimer & Adorno, 1947; Marcuse, 1964; von
Wright, 1986), equating instrumentally relevant aspects with culture uncritically
reproduces rather than explores a dominant feature of culture. Thus not only
what is focused upon – instrumental values and norms – but also the very
framework guiding research reproduces and reinforces a kind of thinking in
which instrumental rationality is taken for granted. These two deficiencies of
current organizational culture research – the focus on instrumentality and the
tendency to take Western managerial and organizational culture as given – then
clearly merge on this vital point. If this tendency can be avoided, then perhaps
the narrow focus on instrumental aspects of corporate culture could be preven-
ted: the preoccupation with such aspects would be recognized as a cultural
phenomenon, and thus not accepted as a natural and self-evident guide-line for
research.

One major rationale for addressing the cultural aspects of organizations is the prospect of achieving a better understanding of 'self-evident' organizational and managerial patterns. Researchers are expected to distance themselves from the phenomena under study and to ask why (cf. Deetz & Kersten, 1983). This could also be done within a functionalist perspective and in instrumentally oriented studies. Schein (1985), for example, suggests that a methodology for cultural studies could include looking for 'surprises' in the culture – things that are different from what the outsider expects. The things that surprise a researcher with a pragmatic orientation are not necessarily the same things that an anthropologically oriented researcher would regard as 'surprising'. The latter would be inclined to view the modern business and organizational world as rather odd and strange in its very nature. The somewhat obsessive preoccupation with profit, economic growth, higher wages, and increased consumption in the world's richest countries, for example, might well appear surprising and calling for careful investigation. Distancing does not of course mean that the researcher must employ 'objective' methods such as questionnaires – the basic approach should be 'interpretive' and should combine closeness and distance in relation to the subjects (Smircich, 1983b) – but simply accounting for subjective meanings is only half the research job. Many interpretively oriented scholars stop here rather than going on to place meanings and symbols in a broader cultural perspective. As Deetz and Kersten (1983: 160) express it: 'To understand organizational reality, then, is to ascertain why a particular meaning system exists by examining the conditions that necessitate its social construction and the advantages afforded certain interests.' Here we have history, language, ideology, and material practice as possible conditions worthy of investigation. These patterns of meaning are better understood if they are approached from a wide spectrum of reference points by a researcher who is both close to and distant from the subjects of the study. Such distancing can be achieved by way of broad theoretical knowledge and reflection and at the same time a kind of naïveté. Those aspects of an organization's life which its members take for granted, not only as a result of socialization and everyday experience in the particular organization but also because they are members of society, should be the targets of research interest.

Eye-opening studies

A few studies in the organizational culture literature do encourage us to perceive organizations in novel ways. One of these is Goffman's (1961) classic study of psychiatric hospitals. Goffman views the social order and all of the practices of the hospital as phenomena in need of explanation/understanding. He does not limit his study to phenomena expressing the parts of a culture that are supportive of the functions and goals of the hospital, nor does he take these for granted. Rather, he regards the very existence of a mental hospital – the assembling of thousands of people labelled 'crazy' in a strange setting which makes them even crazier, all in the name of 'medical care' – as 'peculiar'.

Another is a study by Feldman and March (1981) of the meaning of information in organizations (and in the purposive-rational sectors of Western society as a whole). These researchers suggest that preoccupation with information is widespread not for any instrumental-rational reason but because of the cultural value attributed to information. Information symbolizes reason, reliability, security, even intelligence and is thus a matter of legitimation: 'Using information, asking for information, and justifying decisions in terms of information have all come to be significant ways in which we symbolize that the process is legitimate, that we are good decision makers, and that our organizations are well managed' (p. 178). Paradoxically, it is the cultural value placed on instrumental rationality – on reason, 'facts', and the other things that information symbolizes – that accounts for deviation from the ideal. In other words, people emphasize information far more than is required from an 'objective', instrumental-rational point of view. (Instrumental rationality here of course does not include the tactically correct behaviour of creating the right image or being on the safe side; it concerns productive rather than symbolic considerations. The paradox cannot be resolved sematically.)

A third is Schwartz's (1988) discussion, drawing upon psychoanalytic theory, of the space shuttle as a national and organizational symbol. Focusing on the Challenger disaster and interpreting NASA's symbolic function with ('narcissistic') American culture, Schwartz points to the change in the symbolic function of manned space flight from the 'single-combat warrior', the brave, competent man who symbolically stood for the United States against the Russians (the competitor, enemy) and for virtue ('the Right Stuff'), to the denial of difference. Of the individuals chosen for the trip, five were men, two women, one black, one Oriental, two rather young, one a bit older, one Jewish, and so on; one of the women was a teacher, and the idea was for her to conduct classes in space (transmitted back to Earth via television). Schwartz writes of a picture of the seven shuttle astronauts, all smiling in identical coveralls bearing the NASA logo, standing with the American flag in the background and a model of the space shuttle on a table next to them,

> The picture sings to me: look what America has done! America has transcended its cleavages, men and women fly together, the races fly together, the ages fly together. Even the children can fly. We are all up there in a machine that manages to be, at the same time, powerful and thrusting, like a phallus, and warm and comforting, like a womb. Earthly cares are overcome. Earth and care are overcome. There are

no limits to what Americans can do. Constraint is merely an illusion. I feel on the edge of immortality itself. (Schwartz, 1988: 5)

The mass media focused on the teacher, who soon became the most salient symbol for the project. Everyone has had a teacher, and children still do; the teacher mediates between adult and child worlds. In expressing a childlike idealization of the project and its 'magic', the teacher stood for and, through the mediation of the mass media, encouraged a regressive attitude to the project. Another important aspect of the particular teacher chosen for the job as a symbol was that she was 'the girl next door' (p. 12).

> Her selection, in other words, expressed the message that the American public did not have to do anything to experience utopia in space, but that they could do it just as they were. Americans were telling themselves through the medium of McAuliffe [the teacher] that they did not have to do anything in order to attain the ego ideal, to be perfect – they already were perfect and it was only their temporary boundedness to the world that caused their anxiety. Spaceflight is simply the realization of that perfection.

These types of fantasies – drawing upon a denial of an American society with race conflict, problematic sexual relationships, widespread poverty, and homelessness, etc. – represent, according to Schwartz, a denial of the difference between symbol and reality. Elements of primitive regression were central to the project. Narcissistic fantasies about perfection, magic, denial of problems, and being in the centre of a loving world – fantasies shared by the nation and even more by the organization in charge (NASA) – seem to have contributed to the project's sad outcome. In retrospect, the Challenger project was seen as having been characterized by lack of pressure for maximal competence, neglect of indications of problems, miscalculations of risk, and so on – factors important for understanding the disaster. As Schwartz (1988: 19) puts it, these were 'problems which were always there ... [and] were never thought to matter very much. Within the context of our narcissism, these problems have come to seem insurmountable. Rather than giving up the narcissism and attempting to grapple realistically with these problems, we have given up realism and reinforced our narcissism.' The regression in the organizational culture of NASA can be seen as a significant element behind the tragedy.

A fourth eye-opening study is an overview article by Mills (1988) on organization, gender, and culture. Mills points to 'the ignoring and marginalization of culture' in organizational analysis and argues that sex discrimination 'is embedded in cultural values that permeate both organizations and the concept of organization itself' (p. 352). He discusses discrimination in 'a number of overt (low pay and low authority status) and covert (images of domesticity and sexuality) forms that serve to constrain female opportunity, not only within, but in access and recruitment to, organizations' (p. 361). A cultural system which associates women with 'domestic life' and men with 'public life' restricts entry to jobs or channels women into a narrow range of occupations, normally of a caring or domestic type, serving (superior) men. Organizational culture is (normally) male dominated, involving notions of gender and sexuality in language, stereotypes, values, beliefs, and assumptions.

Still another such study is Ouchi's (1981) comparison of US with Japanese organizations, which offers a new perspective on Western cultural understandings of hierarchy, control, career paths, and specialization. Ouchi's book, however, has a number of drawbacks from this perspective. Its many prescriptions for success tend to 'freeze' thinking and inspire instrumental behaviour based upon it. Thus the eye-opening elements are limited to the initial phase in a process of reorienting managerial behaviour (cf. Alvesson & Willmott, 1993).

In different ways these five studies illuminate broadly shared values, symbolism, and assumptions in Western organizations.[1] The common denominator is their concern with indicating the limitations of apparent rationality. Goffman questions why a particular organizational form exists at all. Mills indicates how conceptions of gender penetrate organizational cultures and how (despite meritocratic rhetoric) gender assumptions guide social relations and lead to discrimination. Ouchi illuminates how managerial principles, far from representing rationality, are located in a particular cultural context and possibly self-defeating. Feldman and March and Schwartz show how symbolism steers thinking and feeling away from what is functional, reflective, and psychologically mature – how mastery of information serves as a surrogate for reason and narcissistic fantasies to some extent 'replace' critical thinking and competence as a governing force.

Anthropological studies of organizations which have the objective of investigating basic values can in fact be seen as dealing with rationality in a critical way: showing what is behind this notion, illuminating its relative and often ethnocentric character and its subjectivity in terms of means (e.g., overreliance on information, anti-social technocratic management practices), social relations (e.g., covert gender discrimination), and aims (e.g., having total institutions control the mentally ill, 'solving' American problems by projecting a false image into outer space).

Methodological suggestions

Organizational culture researchers' lack of distance from managerial/business culture makes it difficult for them to look with fresh eyes upon phenomena and practices that seem natural to 'the natives' and ask themselves, 'What do they think they are up to?' This ability is partly a matter of creativity (which will not be treated here) and partly one of socialization. Scholarly socialization, which clearly differs from the kind that leads to full acceptance and internalization of general managerial culture, might be regarded as a prerequisite for the adoption of a cultural approach to organizations. The extent to which academic training for management research and teaching constitutes such socialization may be open to question.

In ethnographic work within anthropology, the initial difference between the traditions involved (the researcher's and that of the object of study) may produce a breakdown in understanding, 'a lack of fit between one's encounter with a tradition and the schema-guided expectations by which one organizes experience' (Agar, 1986: 21). The researcher deals with this by investigating the cultural elements which are causing the breakdown and then adjusting his schema. Breakdowns continue to appear until the researcher fully understands the culture under study, and therefore ethnography can be described as 'a process of coherently resolving breakdowns' (p. 39). When studying relatively familiar phenomena such as the organizations and managements of one's own country, the problem is not resolving breakdowns but *creating* them. In the study of foreign cultures breakdowns occur automatically, but in one's own they are mostly marginal. The trick then is to locate one's framework (cultural understanding) *away* from the culture being studied, so that significant material to 'resolve' emerges. The problem – and rationale – for organizational culture studies is to turn the well known and self-evident into the exotic and explicit – to raise and answer the question 'What does it mean (apart from the obvious)?' (Asplund, 1970). This is of course to a large extent a matter of creativity, but it is also a matter of aspiring to 'anthropological' rather than technical/pragmatic results. To some degree it is a matter of using the 'critical strategy of defamiliarization': 'Disruption of common sense, doing the unexpected, placing familiar subjects in unfamiliar, even shocking, context are the aims of this strategy to make the reader conscious of difference' (Marcus & Fischer, 1986: 137).

Creating distance

A very simple way in which students of management and organization could look at the objects of their study with fresh eyes, would be to invite people who are not business or organization researchers to participate in the research. Management and organization researchers 'know' what business and organizations are about; they have specific ideas about what to look for and are consequently unlikely to discover anything new in an anthropological sense. Distance is of course not the sole issue for cultural research; empathy and understanding of what is on the natives' mind are also crucial, and these are greatly facilitated by knowledge and insight about the setting.[2] Outsiders might, however, be included in the research team. Another possibility would be for researchers to compare experiences from different (national) cultures (Boyacigillar & Adler, 1991). Some of the advantages of this approach are illustrated in a study of Polish, US and Swedish organizations by Czarniawska-Joerges (1988b), and Ouchi's (1981) study also contains interesting insights. Personal cross-cultural experiences may be as effective in this regard as systematic cross-cultural research projects. Besides experience of different countries, such experiences might include, for example, a working-class background or work as a woman in a male-dominated organization.

These suggestions differ substantially from Schein's (1985) recommendations on insiders and outsiders in organizational culture research, because by 'outsider' he means the researcher. From my perspective, Schein is not an outsider to (most) 'corporate cultures' in North America. As a management/organization researcher and consultant working within a functionalist perspective, he is likely to have much in common with most professional managers in terms of beliefs, values, assumptions, understandings, perceptions, norms, and so on. Professors and managers belong to the same social class (upper middle), they often live in the same areas, have similar educational backgrounds, and even belong to the same social clubs. Whereas there are certainly variations among managers and between these and management professors, who in turn are not all alike, these differences are normally not so far-reaching as to justify any notion of different cultures. Schein mentions being surprised at the relatively high level of interpersonal conflict in one company and the rather restricted and formalized mode of communication in another, but these are breakdowns on marginal matters. I imagine that most of the activities and cultural characteristics of the corporations he writes about are (all too) familiar to him and his colleagues.[3]

Working with negations

Another way of reducing the risk of cultural parochialism is to broaden one's frame of reference. Instead of reading exclusively (mainstream) management and organization theory, the researcher may gain from studying anthropological and historical texts which illuminate the relativity of present Western society and its business culture. Fiction may also provide a valuable source of inspiration. Especially important here are the insights of creative social scientists who explicitly reject conventional forms of understanding, such as the Frankfurt school (e.g. Horkheimer & Adorno, 1947), Baudrillard (1983) and Foucault

(1980). The 'anti-management' orientation that often characterizes this work is an important starting point for the creation of breakdowns in understanding to be coherently resolved.

Borrowing rather freely from critical theory (e.g., Marcuse, 1968), one might call this use of frames of reference which provide powerful counterpoints to conventional views 'negative dialectics'. Approaching empirical reality not as given and inevitable but as characteristic of a limited phase in the history of mankind – confronting its various phenomena with the idea of very different social forms, events, and conditions – can produce fruitful insights. This negation of existing reality may refer either to empirically non-existent but imaginable social conditions or to phenomena that exist in cultures other than the focal one or in particular spheres of the society addressed. An example of the former might be the study of organizations in terms of communicative distortions (Habermas, 1970), which takes as its point of departure the ideal speech situation, in which all discourses are allowed to be expressed and questioned without any repression or inequality among the participants (e.g., Forester, 1983). Through this negation – 'free', undistorted discourse – a number of aspects that normally go unnoticed or unquestioned become visible and can be recognized as worthy of investigation. Hierarchical relationships, norms for interaction and communication which prevent people from saying what they feel is important, and differential participation by organization members in the definition of legitimate discourse and its conduct can all be seen as communicative distortions and as culture-specific. The tacit and not the espoused is then seen as a clue to the culture. Similar uses of negations to confront prevailing social conditions could involve looking at present-day capitalist, hierarchical organizations from the viewpoint of anti-hierarchical organizational forms (e.g., Clegg & Dunkerley, 1980) or contrasting techno-logical/instrumental rationality with a humanistic, anti-repressive form of reasoning (e.g., Alvesson, 1987).

A dialectical approach to organizations as a basis for reducing ethnocentrism and providing the opportunity for less 'prejudiced' cultural analysis can also proceed from less abstract and more empirically grounded types of negation. One example might be the gender issue, where in fact we can point to empirical cases in which males and females have (more or less) equal positions (Billing & Alvesson, 1993). Instead of taking for granted the reproduction of gender differences in organizations, we could confront the fact that women tend to hold lower positions, have less impact on social conditions in general, and are paid less than men with the idea that equality between the sexes is a possibility or at least a possible ideal. The study by Mills (1988) referred to earlier can be viewed as representing this approach.

The negation of existing conditions has important implications for the analysis and presentation of cultural manifestations. Without the notion of negation, the very fact that sex discrimination takes place would never be recognized, and the division of labour by sex would not be considered worth mentioning in organization research. It is perhaps the rather large number of examples of gender equality that accounts for the interest in gender inequality in society today: these examples make us aware of the arbitrary and cultural nature of gender differences.

It could be added that in addressing gender inequality in terms of access to various positions on the career ladder we are looking at a relatively limited aspect only of the parochialism problem. The ideal of careerism and the more basic form of inequality associated with hierarchical organizational forms and labour markets sometimes tend to be taken for granted in our culture. A narrow form of gender analysis mainly interested in equal access to given career opportunities, may attest to a certain parochialism in a society in which upward mobility is a central and taken-for-granted value.

One example of the insight that can be gained through negative dialectics concerns racism. In a study of female clerical work, Tepperman (1976: 49) reports that 'racism is ... clearly visible to anyone who walks through a big company office. Pretty young white women work as private secretaries. ... Black clericals are mainly reserved for the key-punching room, the typing pool, or the data processing centre – the routine, pressurised low-paid jobs.' The majority of organizational culture researchers hardly seem to recognize such phenomena as expressions of the cultures they are investigating. Either they find them irrelevant to an understanding of the cultures of organizations or they are not surprised by and consequently do not notice them. It could perhaps be argued that the management-oriented studies of organizational culture which comprise the majority of culture research need not or should not deal with such 'socio-logical' issues, but I strongly disagree. Management theory should illuminate management and organizational phenomena of all kinds from various perspectives. Gender and race divisions of labour are partly a function of managerial decisions and other management processes, and their cultural features cannot be understood as 'not management'.

Another example highlights the functioning of management in terms of prerogatives. Reading North American texts on organization management, I am struck by the fact that the sovereignty of management is taken for granted, because in many parts of Europe it is more or less taken for granted that employees, through their unions, will have some say in major decisions. By negating prevailing conditions with an ideal situation (that employees/unions should have far-reaching rights in this regard or that management action should be free of any restrictions) or with the situation in another part of the world, a broader understanding of the assumptions, beliefs, and values associated with management might perhaps be achieved.

A third example concerns symbols of organizational hierarchy. Hierarchies are normally supported by a more or less refined web of symbolism which creates and underlines asymmetrical power relations. Martin and Siehl (1983: 57) report, for example, that

> GM [General Motors] had many rituals that supported the core value of deference owed authority. For example, subordinates were expected to meet their superiors from out of town at the airport, carry their bags, pay their hotel bills, and chauffeur them around day and night. The higher the status of the superior, the more people would accompany him on the flight and the larger the retinue that would wait at the airport.

Merely describing this practice reveals some absurdities from a purely 'rational' point of view, but it might easily be seen as typical and taken for granted were it not possible to contrast GM with other organizations which have no such visible status symbols. The negation here calls the whole notion of reinforcing hierarchy and inequality into question. A Swedish computer consultancy firm of my acquaintance provides a useful contrast (Alvesson, 1993a). This company plays down formal hierarchy and emphasizes equality. Office interiors are more or less standardized, and top management is located on the first floor, close to reception. All newcomers, whether managers, consultants, or secretaries, participate in the same week-long introductory course. More or less institutionalized ironic references to 'giant directors' aim at demystifying the managerial role. This relatively egalitarian company policy is of course not contradiction-free, but the lack of visible status symbols is worth highlighting. Contrasting GM with this Swedish company points up the arbitrary nature of status symbols, making it clear that they are cultural rather than natural.

Adopting a dialectical perspective may make it easier to avoid the trap of looking for and finding neatly organized and well-integrated cultural patterns which do not fully reflect the complexity of a culture. As Ehn and Löfgren (1982: 68) put it,

> There is a risk that in searching for culture patterns we blind ourselves to contradictions, conflicts and everything else that does not fit. But what is there to say that what we are dealing with is one pattern or one structure? Against such concepts as capture wholeness and consistency, we should set the analysis of contradictions, inconsistencies, splitting and dissonance. Perhaps it may then become evident that the world of thoughts and beliefs is characterized primarily by disintegration, by more or less demarcated elements which do not cling together.

Reading between the lines

One final suggestion involves directing the attention of cultural studies away from what organizational participants themselves understand as corporate culture. People normally take the basic aspects of societal and business culture for granted and perceive 'culture' as those aspects that are typical of their company in contrast to general ideas, values, and world views. The more interesting and significant aspects of culture are not fully conscious (see, e.g., Ehn & Löfgren, 1982; Schein, 1985). According to LeVine:

> Many ethnographers arrive at the conclusion that what informants find difficult to verbalize is more important, more fundamental, in the cultural organization of ideas than what they can verbalize. They argue that the more general ideas – basic assumptions – are less accessible to verbal formulation because the social consensus in a community protects them from challenge and shifts the focus of discourse to more specific points that are at issue in normal social life. (LeVine, 1984: 76)

When scholars rely heavily on the (espoused) self-understanding of a group, a superficial and commonsensical picture all too readily emerges as a figure against a ground that is lost from sight because of its very size. People tend to recognize 'culture' as those aspects which they have experienced as relative in comparison with other settings but not as what is common to the overall (societal or late-capitalist) managerial culture which provides the background against which minor company-specific variations are perceived. Therefore it may be wise to look for (deeper) patterns in which people do not readily recognize the cultural element. Approaches wherein the overall cultural characteristics of organizations are not taken for granted – anthropological approaches – may lead to interpretations which illuminate the cultural features of contemporary organizations in a new way.

Notes

1 Other examples of anti-parochial organizational culture studies are Deetz (1992), Linstead and Grafton-Small (1990), and Rosen (1988).

2 'At least as regards the analysis of artifacts and the sensory dimension of organizational life, it seems to me that this position offers opportunities barred to the anthropologist studying isolated and exotic communities: it is unlikely, in effect, that a student of civilizations far removed from his own would manage to "get inside the skin" of the natives ...' (Gagliardi, 1990: 30).

3 My personal experiences of joining an organization as a member or a researcher suggests that most of the phenomena encountered appear to be fairly normal, given the overall cultural context. Few things deviate very much from what would be expected. I never cease to be surprised by the tendency of academics in management

departments to neglect intellectually oriented work in favour of more financially rewarding projects, such as extra teaching and consultancy. Perhaps this is a result of my personal values – I see it as unseemly acquiescence in consumerism – rather than of any greater clash between different 'cultures', and it is not therefore primarily a culturally produced breakdown or surprise.

FOUR

A case for a shift of focus in cultural studies

From the literature on organizational culture it sometimes seems that organizations and the people in them are oriented less towards carrying out productive work and achieving instrumental goals than towards telling tales, performing rites, and inventing heroes. The significance of such 'substantive' activities as productive work, the structuring of tasks, the formalization of procedures, the exercise of 'straightforward' leadership, the technical and bureaucratic control of work, and the reproduction of power relationships is often neglected. It seems to be widely assumed that symbols and meaning in work organizations can best be understood without paying attention to the work context. Paradoxically, the emphasis on instrumental values that we have noted goes hand in hand with a neglect of 'core' or concrete instrumental activities associated with work and labour processes.

The appeal of 'pure' symbolism

Using the culture concept and borrowing heavily from anthropology, organization theorists have discovered new aspects of organizational life to study: jokes, coffee breaks, the way people dress, the functions or consequences of the corporation's Christmas party, seating arrangements at meetings, the 'rite' of firing, the stories told about present and former figures of authority, and so on (e.g. Dandridge, 1986; Dandridge *et al.*, 1980; Deal & Kennedy, 1982; Martin *et al.*, 1983; Pettigrew, 1979; Trice & Beyer, 1984). The content and form of these activities and behaviour often seem to be considered of some importance in themselves, that is, viewed as determinants of organizational life (through their sense-making, meaning-creating, norm-setting, and spirit-enhancing capacities) and, indirectly, as organizational outcomes. Sometimes, in contrast, they appear to be viewed as an important source for the illumination of culture but not necessarily of any significance in themselves.

Many researchers seem to suggest that various expressions of culture are significant to varying degrees in affecting organizational culture and life in general. For example, Christmas parties are seen as promoting integration (Dandridge, 1986; Rosen, 1988; Trice & Beyer, 1984) and drinking beer on Friday afternoons as increasing commitment (Deal & Kennedy, 1982) and organizational stories are regarded as a source of control (Wilkins, 1983). These kinds of suggestions are open to criticism in the absence of careful reflection about their relationship to broader cultural patterns and especially if, as often seems to be the case, all cultural phenomena are seen as important in themselves. Phenomena such as jokes, stories, and coffee breaks may be of marginal importance compared with, for example, the organization's hierarchy and the ways in which work is organized, controlled, and carried out and the meanings and understandings that emerge out of these conditions. (Of course, these meanings and understandings also reflect hierarchy and work organization, thereby affecting social relations and structures.)[1] Hierarchy and work organization do not exist in isolation from the ways in which people relate to formal and material arrangements. Organizational structure is anchored in shared meanings (Alvesson, 1993a; Fombrun, 1986; Ranson, Hinings & Greenwood, 1980). Cultural manifestations such as jokes and stories may be connected to the operations of the company, but perhaps only tenuously. Consequently, there is a risk that interesting but insignificant objects will be overemphasized, resulting in a limited or even biased picture of organizational life. For example, does the annual Christmas party have any significance for the functioning of the organization? Would changes in the party result in changes in everyday organizational life? Although some researchers (e.g. Czarniawska-Joerges, 1992; Dandridge, 1986) appear to think this would be so, I have my doubts. While not denying that certain 'objectively' limited events and situations (i.e., limited in time or scope) can have some impact on people's subjectivity at a high level of expressiveness, I doubt whether this is very often the case. At the very least, careful reflection must precede claims about the consequences of isolated, highly symbolic manifestations, and the relationship between the focal cultural manifestation and other elements of organizational culture.

Not all forms of rites, rituals, ceremonies, etc., should be seen as insignificant in themselves. If the members of an organization collectively take up such a form and give it strong, durable, and deep meaning, it may be highly significant, but I suspect that this will be much more common in religion than in modern bureaucracy. On the whole, expressive cultural manifestations are tempered by the bureaucratic ethos. (Some organizations differ rather substantially from the bureaucracy, and in these such manifestations are more common and more profound (see, e.g., Alvesson, 1993a; Van Maanen & Kunda, 1989).)

Within the framework of such a study of interesting cultural details, there are two ways of avoiding or at least reducing the problem of triviality. One is to construct a creative and interesting interpretation, the point being not primarily to mirror a larger segment of empirical reality but to generate an idea or an insight. The other is reduce the scope of the claim. It is, of course, not unreasonable to study more limited, perhaps even insignificant aspects of organizational life if the limited range of the study is made clear. The risk, of course, is that the whole project may be seen as esoteric and unimportant. Two possible pitfalls are a tendency to view insignificant factors as closely connected to the 'essence' of the organization – that is, to the basic tasks and core activities associated with it – and a failure to clarify the scope of one's approach.

It seems more reasonable to view these minor cultural expressions as important clues to broader cultural patterns or, sometimes, more as examples of management's efforts to control culture than as expressions of culture itself. There are, however, some important problems associated with this approach. Symbolic expressions may be related not to culture (in the sense of some holistic, 'system-like' entity) but to something else. Furthermore, cultural manifestations may not be mutually consistent. A joke or story frequently told may have more to do with an extraordinary event or the very odd behaviour of a particular person than with the spirit of the organization as a whole or of a major collective within it. Rather than representing a broad cultural pattern, a party in a small organization may result primarily from the initiative of one or two persons and bear the imprints of those persons and those who happen to attend it.

Another problem concerns the abstract character of what are identified as core values. For example, IBM is attributed a 'culture with several deeply held beliefs and values (e.g., respect for the individual, encouragement of constructive rebellion, and emphasis on doing what is right)' (Sathe, 1983: 12) – values and virtues so generally and positively described as to be almost meaningless. This abstraction is not atypical of the literature in this field (cf. Deal & Kennedy, 1982; Pascale, 1985) or of companies' statements of their own values (Berg & Gagliardi, 1985). The degree of accuracy of such statements can be gauged by negating them and seeing whether they still make sense. If not, they do not adequately describe the values that the organization 'really' holds. (In the case of IBM, the statements exclude values such as disrespect for the individual, encouragement of destructive rebellion, and an emphasis on doing what is wrong.) Of course, there have been some thorough studies illuminating complex patterns of values (e.g., Bate, 1984 and parts of Schein, 1985). As we have seen, it is important in such studies not to rely on official statements or interviews with top managers but to dig deep. Efforts to capture the values (or other cultural manifestations) of an entire organization easily become abstract and imprecise.

Even if the object chosen – a particular symbol, a value (if it is possible to isolate one), or some other cultural manifestation – is treated in a reliable (and accurate) way, there is the risk that it will turn out to be 'peripheral' rather than 'central' or at best apply only to part of the organization. (Study of this part may be a project in itself, and it is often probably wiser to be content with this, but then of course claims to be studying a 'whole' organizational culture should be avoided.) Organizations are complex entities, and it is not certain that the most apparent and widely espoused beliefs, values, and symbols will cover the overall cultural patterns or even those that are of greatest significance for individuals in understanding their work situations. Culture is often best understood in terms of diverse, even contradictory values and symbols (Martin & Meyerson, 1988). Furthermore, referring to subcultures does not solve the problem of hetero-geneity and contradiction; organizational ideologies can be divided into funda-mental and operative groups (Abravanel, 1983), and there may be contra-dictions among them. Abravanel cites the IBM case, in which the values mentioned above are contested by signs of extensive conformism in the personal styles of the corporation's members.

Given these considerations, the relationship between a particular cultural manifestation and broader cultural patterns may be weak and uncertain. This possibility is neglected in the literature focusing on a single symbolic element. Martin *et al.*, (1983: 439), for example, report that 'stories were selected because they generate, as well as reflect, changes in organizations', but this one-to-one relationship between organizations and stories cannot be assumed. The degree to which a story mirrors an organization must be an open question. An organi-zational story may give us a limited, biased, partial, and misleading impression of the larger setting in which it is told, especially if this setting is equated with the entire organization. It may not represent anything but itself. (Martin's later writings clearly support this view; we have already examined her view of culture as non-order (Martin & Meyerson, 1988).) Another possibility is that stories provide a biased view both functionally and ideologically 'by mediating "realis-tically" between organizational members and their perception of the organi-zation, constructing a reality that serves the interest of only a handful of organizational members' (Mumby, 1988: 114). An even more serious difficulty is interpreting particular cultural manifestations, which are often ambiguous and may contain meanings which point to rather different organizational cultures (see Mumby's 1988: 115–24 interpretations of an IBM story, first described by Martin *et al.*, 1983).

From this we can conclude that in order to get at the 'essence' of organi-zational culture – the meanings, understandings, and symbols that are most significant for members of the organization in developing orientations within their communities and work settings – great care must be taken to include those expressive and symbolic forms that have a cultural referent, that can be related to as a cultural 'whole'.[2] Where the researcher prefers a more fragmented, post-modernist picture of the cultural aspects of organizations (see, e.g., Calás & Smircich, 1987; Linstead & Grafton-Small, 1990), the assumption that a cultural manifestation will reflect a broader totality becomes even more dubious.

It is, of course, very difficult to find a basis for distinguishing between 'significant' or 'substantive' symbolic and cultural phenomena and phenomena of less importance. This problem must be solved on a case by case basis.[3] One possible way of developing criteria of some general use would be to proceed from what is significant for members of the organization in their working lives. Symbols or beliefs and values that are unrelated or related very loosely to the concrete job situation might then be considered as not necessarily very significant. It is not always obvious how cultural phenomena are linked to the work situation. These links may be very indirect, but unless they are specified the validity of the expressions and forms being studied will be questionable.

Within this framework, some aspects of culture would appear to be of particular interest for illuminating the 'whole' of the organization from a cultural perspective. Among these I would include basic beliefs, values, norms, and symbolic features of social relations such as influence, privilege, the division of labour, the conduct of social relations, technologies, and the structuring of the job situation. Even though it is wise to reserve the culture concept to the ideational, there is no reason it cannot be used to address the symbolism associated with social structure and material conditions.

The view of cultural patterns within an organization that one obtains from studying typical work activities and examining the values/beliefs expressed by these activities seems to cover more vital ground than focusing on off-the-job behaviour and events. The somewhat exaggerated interest in the latter is probably due in part to the striking features of some of these events (e.g., ceremonies, rites) and the very appealing picture of life in a corporation that is created by a focus upon them (Deal & Kennedy, 1982). Further, with these striking features it is possible to get a glimpse of 'culture' without spending a long time conducting anthropological studies of the patterns identifiable in various types of events, activities, and verbal forms (see Trice & Beyer, 1984). Studying situations and manifestations which exhibit relatively 'strong' and 'clear' meanings, expressiveness, and symbolism is certainly an important part of cultural research, but it must be complemented by study of those (more significant) aspects of organizational life in which symbolism does not appear in so straightforward a form.

Cultural/symbolic analysis of aspects of events, acts, and conditions that were not earlier understood in cultural terms has increased understanding of those aspects and produced significant scientific contributions (e.g., Feldman & March, 1981; Pfeffer, 1981), but, once again, many of these studies tend to overstress the symbolic (cf. Morgan, *et al.*, 1983). Drawing on what participants in an academic conference on 'organizational symbolism' agreed upon, Daft (1983) gives the following examples of symbols within organizations: corporate anniversary celebrations, receipts (evidence of expenses), organization charts, annual reports, company logos, and stories and myths. It is questionable whether the symbolic nature of several of these examples is of any particular significance or interest. In a sense, all social phenomena are or could be said to be symbolic. The issue is whether it is of interest to treat them as such.[4]

Many writers seem to be enthralled by the idea of calling activities 'rites'. Trice and Beyer (1984: 1985) speak of rites of passage, degradation, enhancement, renewal, conflict resolution, and integration, and a very large number of phenomena appear to be 'rites' of one of these types. Collective bargaining and arbitration are examples of rites in conflict reduction. When these rites fail, 'a strike provides another ritualized way to reduce aggression and conflict' (Trice & Beyer, 1984: 662). Without denying that there may be a strong symbolic element in a strike and that there may even be strikes containing ritual elements (at least if they embrace repetitive patterns and if the 'symbolic outcomes' [feelings and attitudes] are as significant as the 'objective' results), Trice and Beyer's use of the concept makes the reader wonder if there are any events of importance in organizations other than rites. A strike is often an important event, but it is doubtful whether the ritual aspect of it is normally very significant. Looking at phenomena from a 'new' perspective, the culture/symbolic one, these researchers often emphasize their peripheral aspects and tend to lose sight of their essentially 'non-symbolic' character.

Seeing many things as symbols is an important means to new knowledge, and it is difficult to make any general statement about what is peripheral and what is not. Drawing attention to the danger of overusing the culture concept simply serves to encourage reflection on how cultural research should be structured. One reasonable conclusion is that researchers should be somewhat more restrictive in their approach. For example, a more careful and rigorous use of the concept of 'rites' would exclude meetings, events, procedures, etc., with clear instrumental purpose and substantive results, restricting it to phenomena whose instrumental functions are limited and subordinated to symbolic ones (cf. Pfeffer, 1981). Readers would benefit from explicit accounts of the considerations which guide the use of concepts, for example, hints on when it is useful to interpret an event as a rite and when it is not. Discussion of the weakness of the concepts used might also be valuable.

Some of these problems follow from the seductiveness of anthropological concepts (Helmers, 1991). They are also associated with an open-minded approach to the discovery of something new in which caution is not a primary driving force. Rather than limiting the scope of the cultural approach, it is more reasonable to shift its focus from the peripheral aspects of organizational life to the activities central to the work of the organization. Organizational culture research should benefit from less attention to 'pure' symbols loosely linked to everyday social and material conditions and more attention to the latter, where the culture approach can illuminate the more important aspects of organizational life.

Taking work into account

A redirection and extension of a cultural approach would cover potentially more important aspects of organizational life than have so far been considered:

> In anthropology, where the concept is most fully developed, culture concerns all aspects of a group's social behaviour.... Applying this anthropological approach in corporations leads one to study participants' views about all aspects of corporate experience. These would include the work itself, the technology, the formal organization structure, and everyday language, not only myths, stories, or special jargon. (Gregory, 1983: 359)

It is of course impossible to consider all aspects of organizational life at once, but it is important to avoid a systematic selectivity that neglects the central dimensions of organizational life. Cultural manifestations are 'not generated in a socio-economic vacuum, but are both produced by and reproduce the material conditions generated by the political and economic structure of a social system' (Mumby, 1988: 108). In particular, the type of work people are engaged in and the conditions under which it is carried out are major aspects and determinants of cultural phenomena. Job content, work organization, level of skills, hierarchical position, differential opportunities, and the demands and patterns of interaction in different groups and strata should all be carefully considered.

Focusing on the cultural aspects of people's work situations may lead to reduced interest in phenomena such as stories or jokes. While concrete activities may be assumed to have considerable effects on (without determining) values, beliefs, cognitive styles, opinions about work and its goals, the company, management, etc., these activities should be seen as central and in many cases given priority over 'pure' symbolism in organizational culture studies. From organizational and work psychology we know (or believe that we know) that, among other things, the content of work, including its skill level, variety, scope, degree of freedom, and perceived significance, is important for job satisfaction, motivation, mental health, and off-the-job behaviour (Gardell, 1976; Hackman *et al.*, 1975; Kohn, 1980). The intellectual complexity of work content seems, for example, to affect values on authoritarianism and belief in the possibility of influencing one's life situation (Kohn, 1980). There is also some evidence that the degree of discretion in the job has an impact on the general level of activity/passivity in and outside the workplace (Gardell, 1976; Karasek, 1981; Westlander, 1976). These simple, basic types of influences indicate that the material aspects of situations affect the cultural characteristics of the workplace. As Young (1989: 201) puts it:

> it is precisely at this level of everyday, at the level of the detailed social processes informing relationships between organizational interests, that the content of organizational culture is continuously formed and reaffirmed. What appears as prosaic detail is actually the development of norms and values whereby events and relationships in the organization are given meaning. The mundanity of the everyday is an illusion, for it is within these details that the dynamics of organizational culture come into being and use.

Van Maanen and Barley (1985: 35) suggest that cultural patterns 'cease to exist unless they are repeatedly enacted as people respond to occurrences in their daily lives'.

Whereas culture can be seen as the medium through which people experience their environment and organize everyday life, it is closely related to the material basis for existence – work activities and concrete social relationships (cf. Foley, 1989; Löfgren, 1982). Cultural elements – ideas, understanding, meanings, and symbolism – are embedded in both the material situation and the social structures of organizations. This view does not, of course, suggest that the culture concept in itself covers behaviour patterns, material things, etc. As has been noted above, culture refers to the ideational level of ideas, understandings, meanings and symbolism. The point is that these cultural manifestations are affected by, anchored in and closely related to sociomaterial reality – they are not freely floating around. On a higher level, the task of an organization appears to affect cultural patterns. Hofstede *et al.* (1990) show that four of the six dimensions of the 'perceived practices' which they see as part of organizational culture are related to the organization's task.

There is of course no mechanistic or one-to-one relationship between material and cultural levels. The former affects meanings and symbols, but these cultural manifestations do not simply mirror material and social conditions in a mechanical way. Materialistic reductionism must be rejected. Jones (1983), for example, argues that culture is determined by production conditions and that the ways of regulating exchange between employer and employee are contingent on these. He imagines three types of cultures – production, bureaucratic, and professional

– which correspond to exchange relations and contracts ranging from the simple and short term to the more complicated, ambiguous, and long term. What he means by 'culture' remains unclear; it seems to be simply a mechanical prolongation of the material and social-structural conditions involving certain beliefs and values.

That the social-structural and material context and the work situation affect cultural manifestations but not in any simple or mechanistic way is very clearly shown by Burawoy (1979). He studied a factory on the shopfloor level and found, among other things, a work culture built around 'making out' – managing to produce enough to keep the piece rate. This was not only or even primarily a matter of pay; instead, it was an act, a gamble, which reduced boredom and provided a basis for discussion, jokes, and integration among workers (p. 62):

> Even social interaction not occasioned by the structure of work is dominated by and couched in the idiom of making out. When someone comes over to talk, his first question is, 'Are you making out?' followed by 'What is the rate?' If you are not making out, your conversation is likely to consist of explanations of why you are not: 'The rate's impossible', 'I had to wait an hour for the inspector to check the first piece' . . .

Similar studies of shopfloor cultures have been done by Collinson (1988), Linstead (1985), Molstad (1989), and Young (1989), among many others. These studies often deviate from mainstream organizational culture studies both in terms of depth of method (often long periods of participant observation) and in the picture of organizational culture that emerges. (Of course, 'organizational culture' here is shopfloor culture, something many writers would call a subculture.)

The connection between work content and cultural phenomena may of course be a bit loser and more indirect than in Burawoy's study, where the cultural manifestation is a rather direct response to a boring work situation. In other cases, more complex psychological processes account for the creation and maintenance of particular cultural patterns. Anxiety-producing and stressful work such as that in hospitals (Menzies, 1960), psychiatric institutions (Kernberg, 1980), or social agencies (Sunesson, 1981) may trigger emotional reactions leading to or at least reinforcing, for example, social defence-oriented work practices and organizational structures, rigid attitudes to rules, formal procedures, and the reification of patients/clients. The cultural elements – shared understandings and beliefs – are significant in affecting psychological reactions to the task and mediating the implementation of rules, procedures, and other structural arrangements. (Of course, forms of anxiety other than those directly related to work tasks and labour processes can also affect culture; being in a risky business can trigger collective, paranoically coloured reactions which influence understandings, beliefs, etc. [see, e.g., Kets de Vries & Miller, 1984; 1986].)

As indicated by these examples, different types of interaction exist between the type of work undertaken and the cultural characteristics of the workplace. My purpose here is not to explain in detail the different types of relationship between work (in the sense of job content and other central dimensions of the total work situation) and culture; I only want to stress the importance of investigating these relationships in organizational culture studies.

For exploring the broader social (rather than the individual) aspect of work and work organization, the concept of social practice is fruitful (see Reed, 1985, citing Harris, 1980). Reed and Harris view social practice as consisting of the following conceptual components: (1) the class of action in which practitioners are engaged as members of a community; (2) the networks of concepts which inform their action and endow it with shared meaning and symbolic significance for the community of practitioners as a whole; (3) the common aims or purposes which are generated and developed through the acceptance and communication of conceptual commonality; (4) the resources, both material and symbolic, which are utilized by practitioners in the performance of their activities; and (5) the situational conditions or constraints under which these communal activities, the resources they require, and the relationships between individual members of the community of practitioners which they engender are shaped and directed. This view points to a close relationship between the symbolic, communal, and material dimensions of organizations and is consistent with the position that work practices (type of work, how and by whom carried out) should be part of any cultural analysis of organizations and that, besides being to some extent expressions of the overall culture, they have a crucial impact on various cultural phenomena in workplaces and organizations. It seems highly likely that the marketing research department and the blue-collar workers in the same company will develop at least partly different work cultures, not so much because of the different efforts of the organization's executives to communicate the same appropriate virtues to all concerned as because of differences in work content, labour process and general working conditions. This may seem trivial, but in the organizational culture literature it is not always self-evident.

An example of the neglect of work in organizational culture research is Wilkins and Dyer's (1987: 12) discussion of the availability of alternative 'frames' (general definitions of situations):

> if the task of the organization requires a great deal of specialization, members of the organization will tend to carry with them different occupational group frames and to look to different reference groups for guidance and approval. The occupational

group protection of alternative frames and the consequent dispersion of power in the organization makes it very difficult to create a coherent, integrated culture spanning all groups.

I do not disagree, but I want to draw attention to the fact that cultural diversity is here being linked not to different social practices *per se* but to the recruitment of differential occupational groups. Rather than being seen as produced or reinforced by different work conditions and division of labour, it is viewed as having been created *before* people entered the organization by their earlier occupational experiences. The potential role of the organizational division of labour – which creates tasks, problems, and sociomaterial situations that differ among employees, and which in turn lead these employees to develop different frames depending on the situation confronting them – is then neglected. The neglect of the material dimension is thus clear in the example. That this is not an isolated example is well illustrated by the collection of papers of Frost *et al.* (1985), based on a conference called 'Organizational culture and meaning of life in the workplace', in which there is scarcely any mention of labour processes, work content, sociomaterial work conditions, or anything else clearly related to social practice. When, for example, such physical aspects of organizations as architecture are considered, they are often viewed not as socio material situations – the materialization of former activities, functioning at present to restrict or provide opportunity for action (Österberg 1971; 1985) or to influence ideas and meanings – but as clues to values and assumptions (Deal & Kennedy, 1982; Schein, 1985). The impacts of organizational material structures upon ideas and meanings have not been sufficiently considered (Gagliardi, 1990).

New directions

It is difficult to capture the 'essence' (if there is one) of an organizational culture (or, to be more accurate, the cultural features of a particular organization) only or primarily through its 'idealistic' aspects – the realm of 'pure' symbols. A shift of focus in organizational culture research might draw upon a view of culture such as the following:

> The cultural cannot be separated from the social as an independent system. Ideas and beliefs are parts of material existence and of people's everyday life on the labour market and in 'politics'. Culture is a driving force behind social change; people's consciousness is developed in intimate interaction with social pre-conditions. Material is dead and without impact without its cultural meaning. Material is a base for ideas, but without ideas, material does not exist. (Dahlström, 1982: 143)

The main thrust of research might then be shifted along the following lines:

1   From a purely idealistic orientation to a broader emphasis upon the *material* aspects of organizational life (including the cultural aspects of technology and work, equipment, architecture, etc.).

2   From off-the-job activities such as Christmas parties to *work activities* as the focus for examinations of expressions of culture.

3   From the organization (or a particular part of it such as a division or department) to the various *naturally bounded cultural groupings* within it (social class, profession, department, or whatever) as the point of departure for cultural studies.

4   From excessive concern with beliefs and values to an emphasis on *social practices* as the basis for the reproduction of the cultural attributes typical of a particular natural cultural category.

This redirection would not imply 'objectivism' or avoidance of an interpretive approach. Cultural understanding of organizations demands attention to meanings, values, and symbols. This approach should not, however, be restricted to the study of the abstract, idealistic system of 'pure' symbolism but be sufficiently broad as to grasp the values, beliefs, and assumptions associated with the material and social practices of organizations.

Needless to say, the shift of focus proposed here is not the same as abandoning studies of 'peripheral' aspects of organizational life. Phenomena 'outside' work activities may be of considerable importance and interest. I am more concerned with the lack of balance and, in particular, with the neglect of the link between peripheral cultural phenomena and social practices. I want to encourage studies which examine labour processes and social practices from a cultural perspective and relate the study of ceremonies, stories, and other expressive phenomena to what I suspect to be the 'core' aspects of organizational cultures. A few examples of this latter sort of research may be helpful. Rosen (1985) examined the managerially controlled symbolism involved in a company breakfast at an advertising agency and found that what was communicated sharply departed from the normal bureaucratic life of the organization. The ceremony, then, included a message opposite in form and content to what was communicated in everyday life and thereby obscured the latter. Relating the breakfast ceremony (the 'periphery') to normal organizational life (the 'core') produced insight into the 'true' meaning of the former and its role in the reproduction of patterns of beliefs, understandings, and social relations. Again, in the consultancy company I studied, it became apparent that management's relatively successful efforts to create and maintain a 'corporate culture' of close, harmonious, open and informal social relations and strong ties among all those employed (Alvesson, 1993a) – encouraging a certain leadership style, arranging social gatherings, designing the corporate building in a homelike fashion, and so on – were a way of compensating for the work conditions the consultants faced: solitary work that was difficult for management to monitor, a rather high degree of exploitation, loose structural ties to the company, and an absence of a feeling of organizational identity. Management's effort to influence 'culture' is in a sense uncoupled from social practice but indirectly strongly determined by it, and cultural control emerges as a way of counteracting structurally disintegrative work practices (Alvesson, 1993a, b). Without relating the values, beliefs, and culture-affecting social events of the company to the work situation of the employees, we cannot understand them.[5]

Organizational cultural research, in the midst of addressing organizational men/women as storytellers, humorists, rite performers, and myth believers, in short, symbol lovers (cf. Ray, 1986), should not forget that they are also producers and workers. The latter terms are not normally understood as metaphors, but in the sometimes strange world of organizational culture studies they seem to belong to a foreign frame of reference. 'Worker' or 'producer' might (provocatively) be used as a metaphor to throw light on organizational culture.

Notes

1 The relationship between culture and social structure is well described by Geertz (1973: 144–5), who suggests that we see culture as 'an ordered system of meanings and symbols, in terms of which social interaction takes place', and social structure 'as the pattern of interaction itself': 'On the one level there is the framework of beliefs, expressive symbols, and values in terms of which individuals define their world, express their feelings, and make their judgements; on the other level there is the ongoing process of interactive behavior, whose persistent form we call social structure. Culture is the fabric of meanings in terms of which human beings interpret their experience and guide their action; social structure is the form that action takes, the actually existing network of social relations.'

2 I use this term with some hesitation, not wishing to suggest the existence of any 'objective' cultural reality. Organizational culture is not a simple mirror of social reality but a framework for understanding. It is, however, important to reflect carefully upon the ideas, beliefs, and values that are important as subjects in organizational life and to distinguish between 'key symbols' – symbols that play a vital role in terms of cognitive mapping, inspiring action, or summarizing emotions (Ortner, 1973) – and less significant ones.

3 The researcher may decide *not* to pay attention to a phenomenon in terms of symbolism because it is trivial and/or meaningless (from both a 'conventional' and a symbolic position) or because it is basically instrumental/substantive in character. Significant symbols are phenomena that have a demonstrable influence on people through their implicit, ambiguous, emotive, and partly unconscious meanings (Cohen, 1974).

4 Sperber (cited by Gusfield & Michalowicz, 1984: 421) interprets as symbolic 'all activity where the means put into play seem to be clearly disproportionate to the explicit or implicit end ... that is, all activity whose rationale escapes me'. As Gusfield and Michalowicz note, what is symbolic for one person may be non-symbolic for another. Still, I think it is wise to use 'symbol' as a conceptual tool for making sense of the hidden or latent meanings of an object.

5 The point of referring to these two studies (my own and Rosen's) is not to bring them forward as good examples of cultural studies taking the material aspects of mark organizations. Both studies may be criticized for not exploring labour processes in depth. They do, however, interpret the cultural manifestations expressed 'outside' everyday work in the light of the material work situation of the employees.

FIVE

Sources of organizational culture

In this chapter the question of focus in cultural research will be pursued further. The main issue is: what are the key elements in the production and reproduction of cultural manifestations in organizations? What are the major driving forces behind the shared understandings, beliefs, values, and norms in an organization or a part of it? The question can be discussed on a general level without any more precise definition of, or metaphor for, culture.

I will also discuss various ways of conceptualizing culture in terms of the social level concerned. There are different concepts of 'size' involved in talking about culture – for example does the entire organization or a part of it correspond to (what is treated as) a culture? We can talk about macro and micro orientations to organizational culture. The issue of size or level of analysis, I will argue, is related to the way we see the 'engine' behind cultural manifestations.

Conceptualizations of culture in terms of level

Let us now return to the question of metaphors for organizational culture. These metaphors are relevant not only to conceptualizing the content of culture, i.e. those aspects of organizational culture that are illuminated by the metaphor, but also to the way cultural manifestation on the organizational level can be understood in terms of the different social entities involved. An overview of different formulations of culture makes this point clear. We have expressions ranging from 'the industrial subculture' (Turner, 1971) to 'small group culture' (Schein, 1985). Some authors see organizations as micro-entities embedded in a larger societal culture; others regard the work group as an entire culture with certain idiosyncrasies and strong boundary lines between itself and other groups. Most authors fall between these two extremes. Berg (1982) talks about organizations as 'cultural products', Wilkins and Ouchi (1983) speak of 'local cultures', and Martin et al. (1985: 101) of 'umbrellas for (or even arbitrary boundary lines around) collections of subcultures'.

The expressions used for culture are of great significance. They frame our understanding of phenomena. Cultural studies are very much a matter of discovering subtle patterns, and our conceptualizations must reflect and encourage sensitivity on the part of the researcher. The choice of phrase expresses a particular metaphor of culture and should not be taken lightly. Van Maanen and Barley (1985), for example, explicitly reject the label 'organizational culture' because it 'suggests that organizations bear unity and unique cultures', something which they find difficult to justify empirically. I agree with their hesitation about the phrase 'organizational culture', if it triggers off associations with 'unitary and unique' cultures. However, 'organizational culture' can be used to signal an interest in cultural manifestations in organizations without any assumption about unitariness or uniqueness, but it must then be supported by clear signals against any such connotations.

Approaches to organizational culture can be described in terms of four major dimensions: (1) the degree to which an organization is considered unique and as producing idiosyncratic cultural patterns; (2) the degree to which an organization is seen as a coherent cultural whole; (3) the degree to which it is seen as independent of culture-producing forces external to the organization (societal culture, professional and class cultures); and (4) what is considered the appropriate 'level' for illuminating cultural phenomena (individual, group, organization, society, etc.). The organizational culture literature commonly assumes the existence of a local culture covering the entire organization that is unique, coherent, and independent and strongly influenced by the founder's ideas (Martin *et al.*, 1985). One could argue, however, that an organizational culture can be unique without being coherent or independent – the combination of different subcultures rooted outside the organization leading to unique patterns and dynamics with a strong 'local touch'. (This presupposes that the subcultures interact rather than existing independently and isolated within the organization, for example, in different departments or on various levels in the hierarchy.)

Whereas the phrase 'organizational culture' or 'corporate culture' in itself – when used as an empirical concept (intended to 'mirror' a certain reality) – may lead to assumptions of uniqueness and unity, other expressions suggest other views. The approach to an organization as a 'culture-bearing milieu' (Louis, 1981) is more open-minded and cautious. 'Local culture' (Wilkins & Ouchi, 1983) calls attention to the possibility of an organization's being characterized by a variant of a more general pattern rather than culturally unique and independent. Conceptualizing the organization as a 'melting pot for work cultures' (Alvesson & Sandkull, 1988) also points to the importance of phenomena outside its formal boundaries. The idea of an 'industrial subculture' draws attention to the fact that culture most fully corresponds to a society and that the sphere of industry includes 'a distinctive set of meanings shared by a group of people whose forms of behaviour differ to some extent from those of the wider society' (Turner, 1971: 1). Turner's point of departure is his experience that when 'moving from one industrial organisation to another, it is possible to observe certain similarities' which differ from behaviour elsewhere in society. This macro-level view might be called 'great culture'. It corresponds to a large collectivity, and I use it to refer to macro-entities other than the society as well (e.g., people living in technological-capitalist society or in a particular country, people belonging to the working class or to a specific industrial sector). By drawing attention to the cultural context of the focal object, it encourages a broader view of it.

In contrast to Turner's macro view, the micro perspective of Van Maanen and Barley (1985) calls attention to the existence within organizations of groups which have different backgrounds and professional affiliations and high degrees of internal interaction and consequently share rather little. One might call this perspective 'local culture'.[1] Van Maanen and Barley argue that 'unitary organizational cultures evolve when all members of an organization face roughly the same problems, when everyone communicates with almost everyone else, and when each member adopts a common set of understandings for enacting proper and consensually approved behavior' (p. 37). These conditions are, of course, rare. These researchers emphasize subcultures created through organizational segmentation (division of labour hierarchically and vertically), importation (through mergers, acquisitions, and the hiring of specific occupational groups), technological innovation (which creates new group formations), ideological differentiation (e.g., when some people adopt a new ideology of work), countercultural (oppositional) movements, and career filters (the tendency for people moving to the top to have or develop certain common cultural attributes) (pp. 39–47). They consider their model both structural and interactionist in content: 'theories that treat meaning as pure social construction jump into the centre of the culture-building process and fail to appreciate the fact that people's actions and interactions are shaped by matters often beyond their control and outside their immediate present' (p. 35). They write that 'only when the ratio of intragroup ties to extragroup ties is high will a common frame of reference regarding ecologically based problems be likely to develop among the members of a collective' (p. 34). As a counterpoint to the view of organizational culture as unitary, this remark is important, but it directs attention to highly local (group) cultural manifestations and away from the larger cultural context.

In fact, ethnographic studies typically offer a careful investigation of a limited empirical terrain but do not relate it to the cultural elements shared by larger collectives (e.g., Smircich, 1983b). (Exceptions are typically critically oriented studies which relate organizational manifestations to the capitalist economy or class relations (e.g., Rosen, 1985.) The idea of, for example, an industrial subculture and the possibility of there actually being shared understandings, meanings, and assumptions among broader groups is neglected. An example of this may be found in Wilkins and Dyer's (1987) study of a company called Modtek. Founded in 1965, Modtek had developed strong commitment among its employees, who were very productive and rebuffed efforts by the local union to organize them. Around 1980 this situation changed; productivity dropped, and many employees voted to support a union. Wilkins and Dyer argue that the change was partly a result of the founders' having built a new luxury corporate headquarters building and withdrawn to some extent from daily contact with the workers and partly a consequence of a decline in profits and the ensuing discontinuation of profit-sharing bonuses:

> the lack of interaction with top management made it difficult for the workers to continue to support the view that they were all 'one happy family'. Thus they sought for an alternative 'frame' to understand the new situation. This alternative frame came from previous experience, from union organizers, and from stories employees had heard from friends who worked in other companies. The new frame that emerged was one that emphasized the adversarial nature of employee-management relations as opposed to the more harmonious feelings of family which characterized the previous frame. (Wilkins & Dyer, 1987)

Wilkins and Dyer talk about 'frames' or definitions of situations and view a change in 'frame' as a cultural change. Apart from the risk of trivializing the idea of cultural change, this approach diverts attention from the broader meanings and understandings best understood on a macro level that inform change in 'frames'. One and the same 'great culture' can help us make sense of quite different situations. I suggest that a general cultural understanding of employee–employer relations informed these employees' responses to their close relationships with the founders, explaining the notion of 'one happy family' not as a simple reflection of those relationships but as contingent upon the belief that such relationships are usually not 'family-like'. The high degree of commitment and productivity were based, then, on the broader cultural understanding that this situation was exceptional. When these relations were perceived to have changed, a new understanding ('frame') was indeed created, but this cannot be understood on the group level alone. If the employees had not proceeded from certain general cultural assumptions about normality, they might have defined the situation in many ways – for example, judging their employers frauds (finally showing their true character) or madmen. But after some time of confusion they defined it in a way which was perfectly in line with the general cultural understanding of normal employee–employer relations and called for a union rather than a psychiatrist. The new 'frame' is best understood from the point of view of 'great culture'; I doubt that the people of Modtek had to hear stories from other workplaces to discover it.

As researchers conducting ethnographic work on organizations get close to the culture and attempt to understand patterns of local meaning and symbolism, what is directly in front of them in the form of interview statements, observed cultural expressive events, and other empirical material often obscures the more distant sources of cultural influence. Informants may not be aware of them. Hannerz (1988: 9) points out the significance of indirect cultural influence: 'There are people in the world who engage habitually only with a rather limited range of ideas, drawn from a handful of nearby sources. But there are also those others whose ideas involve them with much more of the world; those ideas may be of more kinds, coming directly or indirectly from more sources.' That people can develop similar ideas, values, and understandings without having actually met is clear from the ease of interaction on first acquaintance with colleagues from many parts of the world at scientific conferences. The common work situation and the shared understandings following from similar experiences, the exchange of ideas, and the development of shared frameworks through international publications produce cultural similarities across geographical boundaries in the absence of direct interaction. To understand the deeper aspects of culture, we cannot limit ourselves to the local level – the ways in which people make sense of the problems they are facing and influence each other through direct interaction. Broader, historically anchored cultural ideas tend to create unquestioned understandings which restrict our autonomy. Variations on the group and organizational levels may obscure these underlying understandings.

The idea of a unique and unitary organizational culture is contested, then, from two different viewpoints: that organizations are basically products of macro-level phenomena (society, class, industrial sector) and are normally similar and that variations within organizations are much more profound than unitary patterns because of the diversity of the groups involved. These viewpoints are not contradictory: for example, some of the social and cultural variations within organizations can often be related to similar variations on the societal level. There are several reasons that it is important to consider the relations between organizations and 'great culture' (national, regional, Latin, Western, late-capitalist, etc.). There is an obvious interplay between these entities in the production of cultural manifestations (Hofstede, 1985). The interesting cultural aspects of organizations are, as we have seen, not necessarily idiosyncratic values, norms, stories, jokes, language, etc., but deeper and broader patterns that belong to a more general business, industrial, or societal culture. The relationship between organizational culture and subculture cannot be well understood if the organization is seen as a container of subcultures. Studies of cultural manifestations in organizations should not take the organization as a self-evident starting point. Organizational (i.e., formal) and cultural boundaries cannot be equated. A further reason for understanding the subcultural nature of all the cultural manifestations in organizations, even those that are dominant and broadly shared on the local level, is that it makes us realize that management's influence is, after all, restricted. Values, beliefs, and norms about work, hierarchical relations, social relations, etc., are to a considerable degree contingent upon national culture, class culture, and the cultures of professional and occupational communities.

As many researchers (e.g., Davis, 1985; Martin *et al.*, 1985) have noted, the view of organizations having unique and unitary cultures is widespread, and it encourages the treatment of their cultural dimensions as closed systems. That people sometimes emphasize the impact of the 'environment' (e.g., crises caused by a changed market situation) on culture does not mean that they advocate an open view of culture in organizations; the 'environment' is viewed here as non-cultural and as affecting organizational culture only through reactions to circumstances and conditions that have consequences for operations. (Some of the recent strategic-management literature has, however, taken the cultural nature of the business environment seriously (see, e.g., Smircich and Stubbart, 1985).) The production of culture in the public sphere, particularly through mass communication (including ideas on management and organization), is of obvious significance: 'The institutional premium is on new ideas, new perspectives, new definitions of catastrophe, new promises of salvation. Attention and consideration are not given to the glance backward at continuity-preserving traditions or to the contemplation of unifying dogmas, but to the hectic production of cultural goods' (Giesen and Schmid, 1989: 80–1). But in organization theory the relationship between 'environment' and culture is normally treated as weak and indirect. Direct and open cultural flows are seldom seriously considered. Research often seems to be guided by an understanding of organizations as 'cultural islands' or 'mini-societies'. These are not very good metaphors because they divert attention from the organization's cultural embeddedness and its open relationship to the cultural aspects of its environment (for a general discussion of the 'mini-society' metaphor, see Morey and Luthans, 1985).[2] The literature does contain valuable counters to the 'cultural island' metaphor. Meyerson and Martin (1987), for example, consider it 'more informative to define organizational culture as a nexus where broader, societal "feeder cultures" come together', and Beck and Moore (1985) use the phrase 'host culture' to represent the societal context of organizations.

In addition to noting the complicated embeddedness of organizational cultures, it is important to realize that there is seldom a simple way of determining how 'feeder' or 'host' cultures should be conceptualized and demarcated. As Helmers (1991: 65) has put it

> Recognizing the contours or drawing boundaries of a culture is not only problem-
> atic in modern organizational settings – there are international, multicultural
> organizations, networks of intermarket relations, transorganizational stock-
> holdings, branches, acquisitions, etc. – it is a problem in the traditional areas of
> anthropological studies as well. Some people see themselves as belonging to a
> uniform, dissociate society or tribe, as the Tolai of New Britain or the African
> Wodaabe would; others assign themselves to certain totems, languages, villages,
> communities or modes of production (Elwert, 1989). The problem of perception is
> the same in both cases.

One way of handling the dynamics between organizations and their cultural environments might be to talk about *cultural traffic*. Such traffic is, of course, not restricted to matters of recruitment, selection, and socialization of newcomers – the aspects considered by the mainstream organizational culture literature. It is a matter of members' being citizens and as such influenced by societal culture. changes regarding environmental protection, gender and ethnic relations, age, attitudes to work, and so on, affect people not only outside but also inside their workplaces. Cultural traffic is a key feature of modern organizations, counterac-ting any unity and unique character and limiting the influence of management.[3]

The (re)production of culture

In anthropology, the commonly recognized forces or mechanisms that reproduce and sometimes create culture include socialization, rites and other culture-reinforcing events, and ordinary social practices (Ortner, 1984) – the first two dealing mainly with the reproduction of culture and the third with creating (other) cultural manifestations. Other elements (economy, power, language) also function as mechanisms for the maintenance (and sometimes change) of culture, and the first three forces themselves overlap: socialization and rites of passage are a clear example, learning the cultural features of a job is another, and the ritualistic element of ordinary practice (such as Burawoy's [1979] game of 'making out' in a factory) is a third. Given the particular conditions of organizational culture compared with societal culture, two other such forces must be mentioned: the feeder culture and the organization's founder and other key figures (or groups).

The organizational culture literature includes studies of organizational social-ization (e.g., Louis, 1980; Van Maanen & Schein, 1979) and of rites, and most researchers recognize the importance of both. Little attention has been directed to feeder cultures and the interplay between organizations and society. Exceptions to this are cross-cultural studies (e.g., Czarniawska-Joerges, 1988b; Hofstede, 1985), critical studies emphasizing the capitalist element in cultural manifestations on the corporate level (e.g., Rosen, 1985), and studies relating organizations to national culture (e.g., Beck and Moore, 1985). Not much emphasis has been placed on social practice. In contrast, an enormous amount of energy has been invested in the study of 'strong figures' (founders and other leaders).

Culture is constructed, maintained, and reproduced by people. It is people rather than autonomous socialization processes, rites, social practices, a societal macro-system, or key figures that create meanings and understandings. Consequently, culture can be understood by studying people as cultural subjects. It is important to remember here that when an older generation exerts influence on newcomers, so that subjectivity – sense-making processes, affective orientations, etc. – is developed in a certain direction (socialization), human subjects are involved, and the interaction process is important. The same applies to the performance of rites and social practices. Creating meaning and making sense implies activity on the part of the subjects. People are thus culture creators and are not simply transferring and adapting meaning mechanistically. But they are also cultural products (Löfgren, 1982); they are formed by culture, as well as by reproducing and forming it. Culture is also a matter of incorporating unconscious elements – traditions, assumptions, etc. As Geertz (1973) has argued, culture is not locked into people's heads but embodied in public symbols, ideas, and ideologies. Recognition of the important role of subjects in cultural (re)production must be accompanied by the understanding that cultural manifestations are strongly influenced by forces external to the subjects 'carrying' a culture and that culture exists prior to and after particular individuals enter and leave the collectivity.

The role of strong figures in culture creation and reproduction

In the literature devoted to the role of strong figures in the creation and/or changing of culture, a distinction can be made between studies of the role of founders during the formative years and studies of the role of managers in subsequent phases in the development of organizations. Subordinates are typically viewed as rather passive and are poorly represented in both types of research. Founder-centred research emphasizes the historical dimension and views culture as a deep phenomenon which is difficult to change. The taken-for-granted level of culture that Schein (1985) addresses, for example, is often strongly affected by the founder's beliefs and values. Gagliardi (1986) talks about the primary strategy of the organization, in which the founder is the key figure.

Authors interested in managing culture often play down the role of the founder and of history. It is obvious, however, that whereas a founder may have far-reaching opportunities for influencing his workforce, at least for a few years, later managers rarely enjoy that kind of luxury. On the whole they are stuck with certain traditions and a certain set of people. Authors interested in the management of culture stress the potential impact of top management on culture. Most researchers who ask whether management can change culture, tend to come up with positive answers, sometimes supported by wishful thinking rather than careful observation (e.g., Kilmann *et al.*, 1985; Sathe, 1985) but sometimes more reflective (e.g., Lundberg, 1985; Pettigrew, 1985). It is difficult to answer the question with empirical studies. Siehl (1985) found that a new manager's efforts to change values in the organization studied had no major effects that could be registered, although they did influence the expression of values. It has been suggested that the important role of managers may be in maintaining a culture (e.g., Alvesson, 1992; Nord, 1985). Schein (1985) has formulated an extensive theory about the formation of organizational culture of which the founder and group psychology are key ingredients. Given the influence of Schein's book, one of the most widely quoted texts in organizational culture research, closer examination of his position is warranted.

To understand a value or norm, Schein argues, one must reconstruct the history of a group. Usually one finds that the norms have arisen from marker events or critical incidents: 'in response to a dilemma confronting the group, some initiated a position or line of thought or stated a value; the rest of the group ratified that response through overt agreement or silence; and the response solved the problem' (p. 167). Important for the development of a group culture is 'shared understanding' – members' recognition of a particular feeling, experience, or activity as common. Schein thus views culture as

> the outcome of group learning. When a number of people simultaneously face a problematic situation and have to work out a solution together, we have the basic situation for culture formation. The process involves a shared problem definition and a shared recognition that something invented actually works and continues to work. The initial ability to share does involve prior cultural learning and understanding, but the new shared experience begins the formation of a new culture, which then becomes characteristic of that particular group of people. (Schein, 1985: 184)

Schein's emphasis on emotional issues – intrapsychic conflict, group dynamics triggered by anxieties and fantasies, emotional regression, and so on – arises from his experience as a psychologist with T (training) groups, group therapy, and other such activities, in which people are supposed to 'work' rather exclusively with their relationships and emotions. It is questionable whether this is a good model for understanding organizational culture. Schein argues that all organizations started as small groups and continue to function in part through small groups within them. He suggests that training groups develop cultures and pass them on to new group members as the 'correct' way to perceive, think, and feel about themselves and the environment. But training groups are basically interested in themselves, not in the environment. The norms and common understandings developed in the group are typically restricted to the specific situation – a group sitting together and focusing on itself. A 'real' culture has broader influence on people. If shared meanings, values, and understandings among a group of top managers were limited to behaviour, feelings, etc., in connection with a weekly meeting or a conference but had no relevance outside that highly limited situation, we might speak of shared understanding of a particular situation but hardly of a culture. One criterion for culture is that meanings and understandings extend across situations. Similarly, with what Schein calls 'the clearest test of culture formation', shared history, the question is whether this history is deep and long enough. Schein offers the example of the member who arrives late for a workshop and has to be incorporated into the group: 'It suddenly becomes very clear to everyone, including the new member, that missing even a few meetings is very critical because so much has already come to be taken for granted. The new member must learn a great deal to feel comfortable in the new group, and many of the norms may be articulated explicitly in order to speed up the process' (1985: 208). But the group focuses on a particular limited segment of the world – itself – and not on the billions of other topics (e.g., eating habits, ideas about adolescence, and meaning attached to the nation's flag) on which values are shared as a result of a common cultural tradition and which newcomers might discuss without major disruptions. Apart from this, missing the first part of a lecture, a speech, a group discussion, or a joke may be enough for people to 'fall behind' and be in need of some explanation in order to 'catch up'. I do not think it makes good sense to say that a group develops a unique culture after just a few meetings. I believe that we use the concept of culture best if we distinguish it from short-term group phenomena and view history as an important part of it.

In a chapter on 'how organization founders shape culture', Schein offers three examples, one of which concerns Jones, the founder of a large chain of supermarkets, department stores, and related businesses. We learn that Jones 'assumed that his primary mission was to supply a high-quality, reliable product to customers in clean, attractive surroundings, that his customers' needs were the primary consideration in all major decisions', that he employed and favoured

family members in his business, and that he believed in cleanliness, personal
example (visible management), innovation, measuring results, problem solving,
competition within the company (except for family members), and centralized
power and authority. We learn of the others in the organization, first, that there
was one 'lieutenant' who shared the founder's basic assumptions about how to
run a business. We also learn that Jones's assumptions about the role of the
family and the correct way to manage were, to a large degree, in conflict with
each other: 'Therefore, many of the members of the organization banded
together in a kind of mutual protection society that developed a culture of its
own. They were more loyal to each other than to the company and had a high
rate of interaction with each other, which bred assumptions, values and norms
that became to some degree countercultural to the founder's' (p. 213). We are
not told anything about the possible group processes which might have led to
this 'counterculture'. (The material appears to come from Schein's consultancy
work rather than from more careful investigations.) Schein also writes that when
the company grew and diversified, Jones 'brought in strong managers and gave
them a great deal of autonomy' (p. 214). He does not inform us what the rest of
the employees and managers did. To summarize, what we learn is that one
person believed in the same things as the founder, 'many of the members of the
organization' developed a 'culture of their own', and other managers were strong
and substantially autonomous. Jones's influence on organizational culture does
not seem to have been particularly strong; and, when it was, it appears to have
been mostly negative (in triggering defensive reactions).

Schein seems to have in mind Jones's great successes and not his nepotism
and favouritism, which were obviously part of the culture (or at least the
organization – we do not know very much about the cultural level) and which
created problems for Jones – for instance that an employee counterculture
developed, and highly competent young managers left the company. Jones had
assumptions, and he was successful; consequently, Schein seems to reason, his
assumptions 'worked'. Culture enters the picture, I presume, because Schein
thinks that group processes aimed at reducing anxiety and uncertainty make
people adopt norms, values, and with time – basic assumptions associated with
solutions. Given the material presented in his book this appears rather speculative.

In fact, Jones may very well have achieved success irrespective of, perhaps
even despite, his impact on the ideas, assumptions, and values of his employees.
He appears to have had novel technical ideas, to have been a bit of a business
genius, and to have kept the company under strong control at the same time as he
allowed parts of it to operate rather autonomously. It seems that he was not
especially skilful in influencing people's values, understandings, and meanings.

Despite its size, the company appears to have been a very simple structure in which the top figure had the key role (Mintzberg, 1983). This interpretation is reinforced by Schein's observation that on Jones's death the company entered a long period of cultural turmoil. Schein describes Jones's leadership style as follows:

> Jones believed that only personal example and close supervision would ensure adequate performance by subordinates; so he would also show up at his stores unexpectedly, inspect even minor details, and then – by personal example, by stories of how other stores were solving the problems identified, by articulating rules, and by exhortation – 'teach' the staff what they should be doing. He often lost his temper and berated subordinates who did not follow the rules or principles laid down. (Schein, 1985: 211)

It is not impossible that this behaviour had a clear-cut influence on norms and values, with the result that people really did believe in the same things Jones did. However, it appears to have been more a matter of direct control, aimed at the behavioural and output levels more than the cultural one. People were wise to obey; otherwise they might run into trouble. This is probably the most direct and strongest message. Undoubtedly, it also has, as does everything, a cultural content – it affects understandings and expectations – but the relationship between Jones's actions and broader cultural manifestations is hard to determine. The anxiety reduction that Schein believes is important may be less a matter of employees' learning from the founder how to cope with the external environment than one of avoiding anxiety for the founder himself.

Some aspects of Jones's assumptions, values, and beliefs were clearly contingent upon the basic work activities involved. His 'primary mission' probably depended upon customers' non-negotiable demands and other market factors – is it possible that he could have assumed that he was to supply low-quality, unreliable products to customers in filthy, unattractive surroundings and that customers' needs should be disregarded in major decisions? There is the possibility of free (strategic) choice in certain regards, but once one is in a certain kind of business socio-material restrictions to some extent follow automatically. In a mine or a heavy industry, cleanliness is probably not of any particular importance; in a hospital or an expensive shop, it is automatically something to be taken seriously. In fact, many of Jones's values are also mentioned in an account of management philosophy in a Danish supermarket chain (Grant, cited in Bakka & Fivelsdal, 1988), where cleanliness, consideration of customers (who are 'always right'), and visible management are also central.

In summary, the case on the whole fails to illustrate or make credible Schein's idea of the role of the founder in forming culture. (To be fair, I must mention that Schein notes that contradictions in the beliefs and actions of a founder may be important in how he affects subordinates.) Even a founder who has so far-reaching an influence on the business as Jones may not necessarily leave a strong imprint on its culture, especially not specifically through his ability to reduce anxiety associated with problems of external adaptation and internal integration. Achieving a differentiated and nuanced understanding of culture will require distinguishing the general influence of founders from the cultural influence (however limited) that emerges from their ability to solve problems and other types of influence (such as their ability to create problems). Schein's functionalist assumptions are called into question rather than supported by this case and the others he describes.

Most people would agree that during the early years of an organization the founder may have far-reaching influence on it, but there is no guarantee that this will be the case. Not all entrepreneurs are powerful persons with great capacity to affect the ideas of others. Strong dependence on customers or other external actors, other constraints, and the relations among members may all affect an organization in its formative years. Even if the founder's influence is strong, it is not self-evident that it has much to do with culture. Of course, all aspects of a company's functioning involve a cultural dimension, but a founder very skilled at communication, social relations, and symbolic management may have a different impact from one who adopts a more traditional business orientation or one who is highly skilled technically and cares less about the cognitions, sentiments, and values of the people in the company. A founder who creates a technically advanced company and assembles people to that end can be said to have created a 'technical culture', but this is more a matter of creating a certain kind of company whose work and the social practices associated with it affect culture. These social practices thus become a better focus for understanding cultural manifestations than a focus on the founder. Finally, even if the founder's influence does strongly involve cultural issues, the question must be raised to what extent this influence is deep and lasting. Under very stable conditions it may be so, but conditions are seldom stable for long in business. Mergers, acquisitions, market changes, diversification, growth, technological change, turnover of executives and personnel, and changes in the 'host culture', for example, must be taken into account. The cultural boundaries between organizations and their environments are rarely rigid, and cultural peculiarities may be rather precarious. Management often has to work hard to maintain some stability. Values and norms such as service-mindedness, cost-consciousness, a cooperative attitude, etc., are not necessarily self-reinforcing.

In the computer consultancy company mentioned earlier, the three founders proved to have had rather far-reaching influence (Alvesson, 1993a). Ten years after its founding, two of them were still active in the company. A variety of conditions had contributed to their being perceived as powerful and positive figures, and they had thus managed to influence rather strongly the first dozen of employees and, through these, the company at large. One important factor seemed to be that they shared a set of management principles and ideas which concerned a more 'explicit' cultural sphere: they considered community, team-work, social relations, communications, shared values and virtues, etc., vital to the company's functioning and made systematic efforts to influence these aspects. The firm specialized not in technical excellence but in managing computer development projects in such a way that their work fitted into the client's organization and was related to the client's business ideas and strategies. This attribute called for competence in social relations: in project management and interpersonal communication. Another important reason for their impact was selective recruitment of subordinates: at least during the first years, it was mainly people with the 'right' personalities and attitudes who were employed. Despite the fact that the company had grown very rapidly, most of the top managers had started in the company during its first two or three years. (An increase in heterogeneity through time could, however, be noted.) A third factor was that the employees were rather homogeneous in terms of both attitudes and age and profession. A homogeneous group with similar orientations is more susceptible to founder influence than a diverse one.

It was also important that the company operated in a rapidly expanding market and was very successful. Success probably affected the *climate* of the organization more than its culture, however, and this makes it difficult to evaluate the deeper and more lasting aspects. The corporate values of openness, a positive approach, and treating everyone as a friend are easier to maintain in a very positive business situation. It is when the situation changes that one is in a position to determine whether these are cultural rather than situationally determined. Finally, it was an open question how long the impact of the founders would continue to be felt. It was clear that with increasing size, internationalization, diversification, etc., the earlier cultural homogeneity of the company had diminished, but on the whole it remained rather idiosyncratic. I suggested that the influence of the founders would remain significant at least within the older divisions of the company for a considerable time but would steadily decrease as they reduced their involvement with it. I do not think that this case is typical, but it is not necessarily extreme. My point is that the influence of founders on organizational culture cannot be assumed. It is wise to examine carefully what circumstances facilitate or obstruct their influence on cultural matters – employees' shared understandings, meanings, values, and beliefs.

Martin *et al.* (1985) systematically examined the impact of the founder of an electronics manufacturing company in California's Silicon Valley and found some support for the 'founder-centred view', but it appears that the case for cultural diversity within the organization is stronger: 'Many of the concerns and interpretations of the founder were not shared by his employees, and those that were could be explained by contextual factors, such as salience and life cycle stage, rather than the unique actions or attributes of the founder' (p. 122). The influence of the founder is, of course, extremely difficult to identify because it varies from one company to another, from one group of employees to another, and over time. The popular conception of organizational cultures as unitary and unique entities created by founders probably does not reflect the typical case. As Martin *et al.* note, many studies 'argue or assume that shared understandings tend to mirror the personal value preferences of a founder. Thus organization is the founder "writ large", without mortal limitations' (p. 100). A 'founder writ large' view may occasionally shed light on cultural manifestations in organizations, but very few founders are especially large, and rarely are their values and beliefs immortal.

Discussing 'how leaders embed and transmit culture', Schein (1985) views both founders and other leaders as influential. He acknowledges that 'the emerging culture will reflect not only the leader's assumptions but the complex internal accommodations created by subordinates to run the organization "in spite of" or "around" the leader' (p. 224), but he believes that 'the initiative tends to be with the leader'. Schein distinguishes between primary and secondary embedding mechanisms. The primary ones are what leaders pay attention to, measure, and control: leader reactions to critical incidents and organizational crises, deliberate role modelling and coaching, criteria for allocation of rewards and status, and criteria for recruitment, selection, promotion, retirement, and excommunication. The most important of the secondary ones are the organization's design and structure, systems and procedures, design of physical space and buildings, stories, legends, myths, etc., and formal statements. Schein pays less attention than others to 'symbolic management'. As we have seen, Trice and Beyer (1985), for example, view management of rites as central, while Pfeffer (1981) focuses on agenda setting and the use of language. Indeed, an overview of suggestions on how culture can be managed includes almost everything from forcing people to behave in a particular way (which presumably over time affects their attitudes) to supervisory training, job rotation, and the removal of deviants (see Davis, 1985; Deal & Kennedy, 1982; Sathe, 1985).

Management's influence on cultural manifestations must not, however, be overestimated. Hofstede *et al.* (1990) found that founders and leaders did not appear to influence seven out of nine of the cultural dimensions (three sets of values and four 'perceived practices') that they examined. Founders and leaders did seem to have influence on two perceived practices: whether people in their organizations were employee- or job-oriented (measured by indicators such as 'important decisions made by individuals' and 'organizations only interested in work people do') and the degree to which the organizational climate was perceived as open or closed (operationalized as responses to statements such as 'organization and people closed and secretive'). Scores on these dimensions 'clearly reflected the philosophy of the unit or company's founder(s) and top leaders as we met them in the interviews' (p. 308). However, it cannot be ruled out that the causality is in the other direction – that the philosophy of the leader is a reflection of organizational culture (Alvesson, 1992). Hofstede *et al.*'s study may be interpreted as indicating that strong figures have moderate or limited influence on organizational culture as a whole.

Selectivity in recruitment is one important way in which management can to some extent instil certain orientations and ensure that its ideas and efforts to manage values and understandings fall on fertile ground; selective recruitment means the creation of an audience that is receptive to management's messages. There are, however, many restrictions on how selective management can be. One restriction comes from a lack of perfect rationality in the process; it may be difficult to choose the right candidates. There are normally biases and other problems in the processes of selection and evaluation. Another restriction comes from the need for diverse qualifications in the company. Different occupational communities have cultures of their own which do not necessarily match that of management (Van Maanen & Barley, 1984). Smircich (1983c) reports that while the executive of a company she studied promoted the slogan 'wheeling together', most members used it ironically – saying, for example, that the company's 'wheels' moved in different directions. A third restriction comes from recruitment difficulties. It is not always possible to recruit the 'right' persons, irrespective of problems of evaluation. According to Schein (1985: 236), in one of his case companies 'the only candidates who passed the interviewing screen were very bright articulate, self-reliant, assertive people'. Apart from problems in assessing these qualities in interviews, one wonders if it is so easy to get enough highly qualified people. The computer consultancy firm I studied – which was well known, had a good reputation, and was considered to offer its employees an unusually good work climate – had the ideal of employing socially oriented and skilled managers and consultants, but this became harder to achieve as the company grew. The number of people with sufficient technical, managerial, marketing, business, and social skills to be subsidiary managers was not unlimited, and heterogeneity among managers and personnel increased.

A major lesson of culture theory is that the collective is central. It is normally more appropriate to say that organizational culture drives managers than the other way round (Alvesson, 1992). This is not of course to deny management any influence on culture; it is possible to be at the same time a product of a culture, to be constrained by it, and to some degree to be able to change or at least modify it. To view leadership as the management of meaning or management as symbolic action is important and fruitful if these conceptualizations are accompanied by insights about leadership as a cultural 'product'. This approach to organizational culture could be called 'management-centric culture', as opposed to 'great culture' and 'local culture', drawing attention to those features of cultural patterns in an organization that are of greatest significance to the organization in relation to its dominant goals, and to those which are most important to high-level participants and which therefore directly or indirectly influence large parts of the organization. Such influence does not necessarily mean that participants share the dominating values, understandings and meanings, but that all these nonetheless make some impact on people's thinking and acting, because people conform to the ideas and demands of an organization elite. Where lower-level participants have values, ideals, and meanings opposite to those of the elite, it makes little sense to talk about an overall organizational culture at all. The usefulness of a 'management-centric culture' perspective presupposes a 'corporate culture' with at least some broader appeal. A basic criterion for the legitimacy of this orientation is that researchers clearly identify the simplifications and omissions it implies (e.g., by pointing out that the potential impact is uncertain and by paying at least some attention to forces that limit the opportunity for management control). Large sections of an organization's employees are quite often indifferent – or only mildly positive – to ideas, virtues, and understandings held or espoused by top management, and in such cases it might be more sensible to talk about a management-centric culture, upheld by large numbers of top and middle managers and by some other people, and to a much lesser extent by fairly big groups within the company who are affected by the culture and conform to it without having internalized it.

The interplay of research perspectives

While Turner (1971) spoke of an 'industrial subculture', many other researchers have argued that organizations are (or have) unique cultures of their own. Still others have maintained that subcultures are much more significant than unitary organizational cultures, and some, accepting the notion of organizational culture at face value, have suggested that these are empirical questions (e.g., Kilmann *et al.*, 1985). Without denying that careful empirical research can provide interesting material for debate (see, e.g., Hofstede *et al.*, 1990), it is futile to expect that 'data' will 'solve' the problem. Empirical material is a function of the conceptualization of culture, and the same data can in any case often be used in support of rather different views (see Deetz, 1992; Martin *et al.*, 1985). Culture is better seen as a device for organizing attention and interpretation than as a starting point for hypothesis testing.

Different views then, on, for example, culture–subculture relations, are a function of different perspectives, and the problem is developing a framework (or a set of frameworks) capable of reading unity as well as diversity and of avoiding reductionism on a 'macro'–'micro' dimension. The crucial issue is not so much choosing the right or the best perspective – although it could be argued that some perspectives are more vulnerable to criticism than others – as developing a reflective understanding of what a particular concept of culture highlights and what it obscures. Here sensitivity is vital. Such understanding can be facilitated by the confrontation of different concepts of culture – not only mastering one perspective but grasping its relations to others.

In a discussion of the relation between the centre and the periphery in the world, Hannerz (1988: 6) describes conventional thinking as follows: 'The center mostly speaks, and the periphery mostly listens, without talking back.' In many if not most studies on organizational culture, management defines culture and – while the rest of the organization may be more or less receptive or more or less conservative in relation to new messages – has a degree of cultural control. The periphery may be deaf or listening without concentration, but an interesting, competently delivered speech which considers the particular characteristics of the audience stands a good chance of influencing those addressed. The periphery never talks back. This is the perspective I have called 'management-centric culture'. In contrast, from the 'great culture' perspective cultural manifestations in organizations are understood as reflections of broader, historically anchored cultural patterns. This perspective draws attention to 'long cultural waves' – to the durability of culture and the slowness of change. Subjects on the local level share many of the overall cultural features as members of a society, a class, an occupational community, a region, etc., but depending on the constellation of groups in the organization and its basic tasks, different elements of the overall cultural patterns are drawn upon and actualized in a particular organizational setting. Although individual subjects are apparently produced by rather than are producers of 'great culture' (as a consequence of the size of the culture concept involved), the notion is not necessarily deterministic. It simply suggests that local phenomena must be understood in this broader context and that culture also affects the unconscious and the 'taken-for-granted'. From the point of view of 'great culture', the organizational level is thus far from uninteresting. Even if the organization is viewed as basically a site for feeder cultures, these may develop particular characteristics in this setting, depending on local conditions.

Local actors are not just passive carriers of culture; the point is that they are informed by cultural traditions which go beyond their consciousness. The interplay between different macro elements may produce organizational cultural manifestations that cannot be reduced to mechanical reflections of broader (extra-organizational) cultural patterns. Thus the creation of meaning on the local level must be understood in terms of input from 'non-local' forces.

While the 'management-centric culture' perspective normally views founders and leaders as the prime movers and the 'great culture' perspective draws attention to feeder cultures as a major source of meanings and understandings, the 'local culture' perspective takes small-scale, 'natural' collective formations as the major culture-producing factor. Culture is here seen as subjects' collective creation of their own social reality. The processes involved are short lived and interactional (interpersonal). People's direct experiences and consciousness – the problems they face, the groups they belong to, and the people they interact with – are often emphasized. The voluntaristic element is strong here. People are viewed as being able to account for how they relate to and understand social reality – making sense of their worlds without being controlled by cultures in a systematic or regulated way. The notion of 'local culture' emphasizes 'short cultural waves' – meanings and understandings are viewed as changing with changed social circumstances. In a stable setting and in a group with firm boundaries, culture may be more stable and these waves longer. While 'great culture' tends to be associated with long and 'local culture' with short cultural waves, it is perfectly possible for 'great culture' to change quickly, for example, as a consequence of mass communication or rapid social change, while a particular local community relatively isolated from the larger society may be very conservative.

Organizational culture studies would benefit from taking seriously all three of these perspectives alongside of the notion of organizational culture as unitary and unique. The point is to be aware of all three ways of making sense of cultural manifestations and let those not being directly utilized enrich the account. The researcher adopting the 'great culture' perspective will clearly acknowledge the importance of the 'local touch'; the 'management-centric' researcher will bear in mind the (often) thin and precarious nature of the unique and the unitary on the organizational level and the normally artificial character of 'corporate culture'; the researcher adopting the 'local culture' perspective will not lose sight of the broader cultural manifestations that are normally the basis for the variant meanings developed by different local subcultures. Studies of group formation, group identification, and interaction as a basis for shared meanings can then be balanced against insights with regard to the influence on these processes and meaning structures of the larger cultural setting (the organization) and the ways in which feeder cultures structure and guide the more refined meaning patterns on the local level.

Notes

1 I prefer 'great culture' and 'local culture' to 'macro' and 'micro' culture for their connotations. 'Micro' is often used to point to a rather detailed level, for example, the individual (Johansson, 1990), whereas the idea of culture applies to a collective (normally not especially limited size) rather than to the microscopic level. 'Macro' is sometimes used to indicate social phenomena above the individual level, for example, the institutional, Ouchi and Wilkins (1985), for example, talk about 'macro-analytic theories' and then refer only to the group and organizational levels. 'Macro' used in this way is not 'macro' enough for my purposes, for I want to draw attention to cultural entities beyond the organizational level. A more important reason for recommending 'great culture' and 'local culture' is that I want to avoid a sharp distinction between the two views which might suggest that they are contradictory and mutually exclusive. ('Macro' and 'micro' have these connotations.) The idea is that these are different but complementary kinds of understandings of cultural phenomena in an organizational context – different perspectives on organizations and different ways of framing the cultural manifestations within them.

2 The societal level is not necessarily best treated as more 'reliable' or 'real' than any other object of analysis. To what extent society is a theoretically fruitful concept or a meaningful empirical entity is open to discussion (Ahrne, 1990). A recent critique of traditional understandings of macro-sociology makes the point that 'the macro appears no longer as a *particular layer* of social reality on top of micro episodes. . . . Rather it is seen to reside *within* these micro episodes where it results from the *structuring practices* of agents' (Knorr-Cetina, 1981: 34). My position is that we must avoid reification of any of the various 'entities' or levels important for cultural studies of organizations. Drawing attention to macro-level entities such as society, industry, and class will allow us to understand local phenomena in a certain light but not to reduce them to reflections of more 'real' macro- structures.

3 Total organizations are an exception to this; some organizations which have only or mainly an internal labour market, such as the police and the military, many Japanese industries, and, to some extent, certain Western industries recruiting mainly from within are characterized by a rather low degree of cultural traffic, although cultural change in society certainly affects these organizations as well. Cultural traffic goes not only from 'society' (societal spheres outside the formal organization focused upon) to the organization but also in the opposite direction. Society is made up of organizations; as Perrow (1986) puts it, 'the major aspect of the environment of organizations is other organizations'. For the individual organization, its environment influences it more than the other way around; in other words, it is the environment rather than the organization that directs the traffic.

SIX

Cultural homogeneity and heterogeneity in a university department

Some of the ideas discussed in the preceding chapters may gain substance from an account and interpretation of a case study. The organization in question was a medium-sized department at a major Scandinavian university. Its purpose was instruction and research in applied and clinical psychology. The staff consisted of about twenty-five employees (active in the department on at least a half-time basis) and some additional persons with a more peripheral connection with the department. In addition there were about 200 students. About half of the department's employees had been chosen for their practical experience (mainly in psychotherapy), which was considered important for teaching; most of these were part-time lecturers. The other half had mainly academic credentials. Most of them were over forty, and half of them were over fifty.

The department had been founded at the beginning of the 1970s, largely in response to a lack of interest on the part of the country's university departments in psychology in the development of applicable knowledge. The tense relationship with representatives of the broader discipline had been an obstacle to the establishment of the new department. Because it is difficult to maintain complete anonymity for the organization, I wish to emphasize that the information and analysis reported here apply to the mid-1980s.

I was associated with the department, with occasional interruptions, for six years, first as an undergraduate and Ph.D. student and then as a teacher and researcher. Throughout the period I was also active in other organizations, mainly academic in nature. On several occasions I worked at universities abroad, and after leaving the department I held positions at two other universities. This background afforded closeness to the object of study and the possibility of ample observation and at the same time a certain distance; to some extent I was able simultaneously to occupy outsider and insider positions. In any case, my socialization into the organization should not have led to blindness to conditions within it.[1] Organizational culture research demands a particular combination of closeness and distance (Schein, 1985; Smircich, 1983b), and my belief that I possess such in this case contributed to my interest in conducting the study.

There are, of course, problems associated with this type of effort. One of these is that most of the observations were made consecutively and unsystematically. Selective perception of data and tendentious interpretation are risks of which I am very well aware. Another problem is a lack of neutrality with regard to the organization in question. The degree of personal involvement is, obviously, much higher than in conventional research. I have tried to reduce the import-ance of my own excess subjectivity and the risk of being misled by unsystematic observations by checking my understandings with members of the department. Five senior members read and commented on various drafts of this chapter, and consideration has been given to their opinions. On the whole, they confirmed my analysis, and their comments have been incorporated into the text.

Cultural characteristics of the department

The department was characterized by a rather tolerant attitude towards others. The atmosphere was friendly and relaxed. Compared with various other places of employment it had little internal criticism, slander, or malicious joking. Conflict was avoided partly by avoiding discussion of ideals and standards. People were somewhat cautious about making demands. Social pressure to perform according to defined standards or to attain particular results was not as evident as is normally the case in academic contexts. Values such as prestige and status were less often expressed. Rivalry with respect to knowledge, achieve-ment, and success was, with few exceptions, limited. Little was said about whether anyone functioned well or poorly as a researcher, teacher, or pro-fessional psychologist. Members of the department did not, on the whole, appear to think it important to defend their positions with regard, for example, to scientific, pedagogical, or practical-psychological achievements or to give the impression of being well read, progressive, original, creative, or any of the other things that are often accorded prestige at universities. The content and quality of the research reports produced in the department and periodically distributed to all personnel did not seem to be made the subject of discussion, comment, or speculation, nor was the quality of the (few) dissertations presented widely discussed. Lack of interest in what others were doing (or not doing) was rather widespread. The 'right' attitudes and preferences were, however, important to many people; psychology, and about half the personnel had invested a great deal of energy in these fields.

Instruction was characterized by few demands. Teachers of practical courses declared that it was impossible to fail students, but even in 'theoretical' courses failure was unusual. Students, for their part, felt that instruction was too diverse – that teachers did not present a uniform line. When I asked ten students, each with about two years' experience in the department, to write about the features they considered to distinguish the department as an organization – its overall patterns, 'culture', or 'style' – they reported perceptions of 'a lack of a common line', 'poor administration', 'widespread confusion', 'no demands', and 'no uniform general conditions with respect to the subject and to the students'. An important shared understanding appears to have been that it was difficult to evaluate this type of education – to establish clear criteria for 'achievement'. Teachers sometimes discussed students who appeared to be very ill-suited to the role of psychologist, but these discussions normally ended with references to difficulties in evaluating and in undertaking 'corrective' action.

At the same time, it was agreed that the department was engaged in something special and unique which outsiders did not understand. (Sometimes I had the feeling that the department's members did not understand it either.) The environment was considered threatening. The prevailing view was that the unique character of the department's activities had to be defended, especially against 'bureaucrats' and, to some extent, the neighbouring department of general psychology. (This is not to say that the threat of a merger was not genuine.)

The department can be described, with respect to tasks and formal matters, as a professional organization without any pronounced common professional attitude. Widely shared values played down the importance of occupational competence and professional achievement. To the extent that ideas about professionalism were expressed they were rather vague, alluding to the 'right' way of relating to people (consistent with the special demands of the work of clinical psychologists). That the work environment appeared to be difficult to describe in explicit, 'objective' terms and difficult to assess meant that the more codifiable knowledge and explicit achievements were accorded less importance. An account of a special situation in the department – a party arranged in connection with the appointment of a professor – will illustrate some of what I have been saying.

A ceremony

The more profound affective-expressive dimensions of organizations are expressed in symbolic form in which various events, statements, and material objects communicate the common subjective structures which link people together and integrate their activities (see, e.g., Allaire & Firsirotu, 1984; Dandridge *et al.*, 1980; Trice & Beyer, 1984). One such symbolic form is the ceremony, which Dandridge (1986) describes as 'an integration of work and play'. The explicit, conscious meaning of a ceremony for most of those involved is in fact well-being. People are celebrating something: Christmas, somebody being pensioned, a fiftieth birthday, an achievement or award. As do other symbolic recurrent events such as rites and rituals (which are of a more everyday character), however, the ceremony has a number of implications: 'positive' ones such as the overriding of job roles and increased integration with the collective and/or the organization in its entirety and the communication of central values, basic assumptions, and objectives and 'negative' ones such as the reinforcement of the hierarchy of power and implicit communication of the dominant group (see, e.g., Dandridge (1986), stressing the former, and Rosen (1985), emphasizing the latter). There are always problems in interpreting the 'representative' cultural content of a particular expressive situation; it seldom stands in a one-to-one relationship to broader cultural patterns and therefore must be interpreted with care.

With regard to the ceremony I am going to describe, the risk of misinterpretation is relatively small because I have studied the department for a number of years and have been able to observe both symbolically charged and daily activities. My interpretation of it benefits from the background knowledge acquired through participation in hundreds of meetings, planning conferences, seminars, parties, conversations, teaching situations, etc. Everyday life observations of cultural manifestations balance the rather selective material offered by the ceremony, and on the basis of this background knowledge I believe that I can identify those features of the ceremony which are 'culturally significant'.

The newly appointed professor, who had been working in the department for about twelve years, celebrated his appointment by inviting the staff to drink champagne on a workday afternoon. Some fifteen members turned up. The ceremony took place in the lunch room, which became quite crowded. The setting was a mixture of informality and solemnity. People sat on various kinds of chairs, and the sink counter and small tables were covered with paper plates for sandwiches and plastic glasses for champagne. For the most part those present were dressed in typical psychologist's clothing, sweaters and corduroy trousers.

The chairman of the department gave a speech that began, 'Herr Professor', and stressed the new professor's research guidance role. The chairman recollected the subject's arrival in the department as a newly appointed assistant professor, when he had said that he did not know very much about applied psychology but was eager to learn. What the chairman wished to emphasize, he said, was the other man's 'cautious, quiet, and unpretentious manner' – an impression which he had no occasion to revise. He added that the newly appointed professor had always proved most diligent.

A few minutes later the new appointee gave an informal and somewhat personal speech of his own. What he was about to say, he began, would be different from the chairman's 'academic and formal' speech. He mentioned several occasions in the history of the department which he considered 'rather dramatic'. He observed that the department had been founded in the face of resistance from the department of psychology (alternately referred to as 'the department next door', 'the paternal department', and 'big brother'). He himself had come from that department, in which a year or two earlier had taken his doctorate, and he had been advised by colleagues in that department to avoid getting involved in too many 'meetings and groups'. (Laughter was heard from those present.) They had also advised him to see to it that there would be 'solid research in the department'. He spoke of the establishment of the chair and the initiation of research. He pointed to the ninety registered Ph.D. students. After describing how the Ph.D. programme had been established in the face of external resistance, he talked about the plans for merging the department with the department of psychology, which for several years had been a real threat. Solidarity had been strong during that period, he added, and he had met with others on weekends to draw up strategies for defending the department. 'If we had not done so, we would not be sitting here today.' He finished his speech by mentioning something which he considered to be of special importance; 'integrity as clinical psychologists' and its implications for 'attitudes to human beings'. (A background detail in this context is that at the time of its announcement the chair had been given the title of 'Clinical Psychology' instead of the earlier designation 'Applied Psychology'.)

After a final 'Skål!' and a moment of silence, one of the faculty members inquired whether this attitude to 'clinical psychology' included herself and two others, none of whom was a clinical psychologist. The professor replied, gently and tactfully, that the term 'clinical psychologist' was intended to be understood in a broad sense. One of the other faculty members asked, 'This attitude: does it mean being kind?' The comment was ironic with regard to the psychological attitude, which, although somewhat vague and difficult to express in intellectual or scientific terms, might perhaps be regarded as humanistic. In the department there was a certain antagonism between the clinical psychological or therapeutic and the intellectual-scientific. The ironic comment evoked hearty laughter; it was as though those present were choosing between laughter and taking the matter as a provocation.

Two comments were immediately offered in this ambiguous exhilarating atmosphere: 'That was a comment by a non-clinician', remarked the professor. 'Here, as a supervisor, I must intervene and give due warning', said the former supervisor of the maker of the ironic comment, also a non-clinical psychologist and peripherally associated with the department, 'You are cutting off the branch you are sitting on.' With his comment the professor of course drew attention to the speaker's lack of correct attitude and/or knowledge of the clinical/therapeutic activities which many in the department (above all the practitioners/teachers and the professor himself) regarded as core activities. By means of his intervention, the supervisor stressed that this core was dominant and taboo – that joking about such a sacred matter might lead to trouble – and in so doing revealed a certain critical attitude to this. Irrespective of this little incident, the party continued in a rather high-spirited fashion. Many people became slightly affected by the champagne. Most of the guests made their departure after about two hours. By 6 pm only the professor and two of his Ph.D. students were still there, talking about and attempting to interpret their dreams.

Some features of this ceremony, rather than reflecting dominant cultural patterns in the department, were influenced by individual and random factors. Thus, for example, the chairman's opening his speech with the words 'Herr Professor' was not an expression of any formal or hierarchical organizational style, despite the fact that members of the department associated the title 'professor' with considerable status. (In Scandinavia, as in Britain and many other countries, most university teachers are employed as lecturers; a department usually has only one or a very few professorial chairs.) Otherwise, there was much to observe at the party which revealed the character of the organization.

That the party took place at all expressed a certain social attitude; at least some of the personnel desired more social and festive life in the department. (Cakes on birthdays were not unusual, for example.) Informal clothing, crowding, and informal seating were acceptable.

The professor's qualities – 'cautious, quiet, and unpretentious' – were appreciated by all present. If there had been any doubt about the matter – and there would have been in many other organizations – the chairman in all probability would have found something else kind to say about him.

Nothing was said about the quality or content of the research work which must be regarded as an important reason for his appointment and which would surely be essential to his future activities. It may be that no specific insight or evaluation worth mentioning with regard to its content was current in the department, hence the rather cautious and not altogether central judgement that it was the professor's diligence that had prepared the way for the promotion in question.

The informal and personal character of the professor's speech was also in part an expression of some collective appreciation of such attitudes in the department. We realize that he would not have made a speech of this kind in the neighbouring ('big brother') department. At the same time, not all employees shared these attitudes, as may be deduced from the chairman's somewhat more formal speech.

The content of the professor's speech offers many clues to members' attitudes. The problematic relationship with the department of psychology, with its 'big-brother' tendencies, was characteristic of the department during its first years and to some extent thereafter: there was no desire to merge with the other department as the administrative authorities within the university occasionally proposed. The inability of its neighbour to understand the department's activities gave rise to witticisms. The exhortation from the former about 'solid research' in the department can be interpreted in two ways: either this was indeed necessary or such suggestions from the neighbouring department could be taken with a certain amount of irony.

The emphasis on 'integrity as a clinical psychologist' expressed a humanistic attitude to which direct reference was made in connection with the presentation of the ceremony, and here certain tensions came to light. Clinical psychology was dominant and those involved in it relatively numerous. At the same time, there were quite a few other people with different orientations who felt neglected and expressed different attitudes and views. The reactions to the final words of the professor's speech indicated opposition of this kind.

The end of the account illustrates a point to which attention has previously been drawn – the tolerance for personal and emotional expression in the department.

The content of the ceremony, especially the professor's speech, may be regarded as an example of a degree of 'symbolic leadership' (Pfeffer, 1981), the aim being to (re)establish a feeling of community, partly by playing on the unsympathetic environment.

These interpretations indicate that the following assumptions and values were important in the department: an acceptance of the personal inner life of the individual, a cautious, friendly, 'therapeutic' attitude, stress on the 'correct attitude' rather than (measurable) achievement, and the idea that the department was engaged in something special which outsiders did not really understand.

The department as one culture?

To understand this case, we must consider the department's principal task – the education of psychologists. This is regarded as a difficult job, particularly with respect to attaining good results, and opinion is divided on how such results are defined. Many believe that, for example, 'ability to empathize' is important for a (future) psychologist, but it is very elusive. How important is it compared with book knowledge? How much effort should be invested in trying to develop it? Can it really be taught (in an educational institution)? What does it really mean? Is it possible to make reliable judgements as to whether students have attained it? The training of, for example, law or engineering students is obviously in this respect a simpler pedagogical task. Uncertainties with respect to this task and difficulties in establishing and maintaining standards and ideals in various ways had left their mark on the values and understandings of the department's personnel. The idea that it is impossible to make reliable judgements and uphold clear ideals in education was reflected in the overall cultural patterns of the department. Caution, passivity, and an unwillingness to pronounce judgement distinguished it from many other university departments. Thus the specific social practice of the organization – the education of psychologists – influenced its cultural features.

By regarding its members as a collective, emphasizing overall patterns, and disregarding differences within the organization we obtain some understanding of the functioning of the department in cultural respects. It could be argued that the organization concerned is an exceptionally clear demonstration of the existence of unitary and unique organizational cultures. Compared with most organizations, it was extremely homogeneous. With the exception of a few secretaries, every employee had an M.A. or a Ph.D. in psychology, most of them had studied at the same university, turnover was low, and all were involved in teaching the same students. Whether it was unique in all this is difficult to say, but it certainly differed in some regards from other departments and displayed some idiosyncratic cultural patterns. Whereas there are good reasons for talking about widely shared cultural manifestations in the department, however, an organizational-level interpretation is insufficient for understanding it. Elucidation of both the functions of different groups within the organization and the conditions described here requires that the different cultural orientations represented within it also be studied.

Beyond organizational culture

A more profound perspective on cultural patterns in the department draws attention to cultural differentiation. The presence of significant differences was indicated by the assorted reactions to the speech by the newly appointed. professor. The expression 'integrity as a clinical psychologist' failed as a common symbol. Because the notion of subcultures is inadequate and potentially misleading, I shall instead speak here of social fields.

A social field (Bourdieu, 1979) is a distinct field of activity and qualifications with its own rules for success and recognition and its own (often hierarchical) structure of positions and economic and symbolic rewards. A field requires a specific cultural competence, specific investments in views, attitudes, and knowledge, and a command of a particular symbolism. Examples of fields are industrial management, stock speculation, academic psychology, literary criticism, and business consultancy. What constitutes a field and where its boundaries lie are not to be taken for granted but depend on the researcher's construction.

The field, as an arena for work, achievement, and recognition, requires a 'habitus', a structured disposition for perception and action within it (Bourdieu, 1979; Sulkunen, 1982). Habitus is thus a more or less profoundly incorporated competence which is the key to success in the field in question, and this is a cultural competence through which social codes are mastered (cf. Swidler, 1986). To be highly successful in a particular social field, a person must have acquired the right habitus. Habitus in one field does not guarantee successful action in another.

In my opinion, the department can best be understood with reference to two different fields: the practical-psychological and the academic-scientific.[2] Both are ambiguous, and each has variants so different from the other as to make it seem more reasonable to speak of, for example, experimentally measuring and qualitatively interpreting research as two separate fields within the (heterogeneous) academic-scientific field. In a way, the department was situated at the intersection of the two fields; it was a university department with application training as its most important activity. These two fields are in many respects dissimilar (see table 1), partly because academic psychology, compared with most other social scientific disciplines in the country in question, is extremely 'positivist' while many practical-psychological activities stress extremely 'soft' dimensions (e.g., empathy).

Although there are important similarities in terms of knowledge and, to some extent, spheres of interest between academic and practical psychology, the differences with regard to the cultural and symbolic competence required are striking. The central importance of 'soft' variables for correct action in practical-psychological activities, which often include the capacity to make contact, intuition, and an appealing, expectant, cautious, encouraging, empathic attitude, have scarcely any counterpart in (positivist) academic psychology. In the latter it is seldom a question of a long-term focus on the client's (and partly also on the psychologist's) emotional life in an intensive relationship. In addition, titles and other career markers are different. In psychotherapy people can obtain various degrees which are solely dependent on practical experience (e.g., supervised work with clients, self-therapy, etc), where formal careers in research of course are completely different. The 'cultural capital' is field-specific. The characteri-

Table 1   *Academic-scientific and practical-psychological fields compared*

Dimension	Academic-scientific (dominated by experimental-quantitative research)	Practical-psychological (dominated by psychotherapy)
Socialization	For mastery of method and techniques, obedience to explicit rules, independence and creativity within the framework of prevailing research ideals (paradigm).	For fulfilment of 'the role of the psychologist', regarded as difficult to define and involving diffuse qualities such as empathy and self-insight. Also for self-therapy.
Method of work	According to manuals;. minimization of personal influence.	Personal involvement, the use of oneself as a working instrument.
	Explicitly reported procedure in work. Publicity principle.	Implicit, difficult to communicate. Involves private relationship between psychologist and client, secrecy.
Character of work results	Communicated to the research community, assessed through feedback from colleagues (e.g., when reviewing for publication).	'Private', almost impossible to assess. (Colleagues possibly have an impression of psychologist's skill or lack thereof.)
	Relatively reliable criteria for evaluation (at least within a paradigm).	Very unreliable criteria for evaluation. Efforts are very often 'without effect' or lead to results which are difficult to assess.
Formula for success	Intellectual capacity. Knowledge of theory and method. Achievements via publications.	Style, personal appearance indicating knowledge of people, emphatic capacity.
Standards, ideals	Relatively unambiguous and easy to formulate.	Unreliable, diffuse.

zations in table 1 nicely fit conventional understandings (stereotypes) of masculinity and femininity, respectively; in terms of values and style there is a rather strong gender division between the two fields. In the department as well as in general, representatives of the academic-scientific field are mostly men, while women are in the majority in the practical-psychological field. This gender aspect further underscores the differences between the two.

The department was thus characterized by the presence of two different cultures that had their origins outside it. They were occupational cultures, and their range extended far beyond the department. However, the broad patterns illuminated by this 'great culture' perspective were not mechanically mirrored at the local level. From a 'local culture' point of view, each of the two fields was heterogeneous. Within the academic-scientific field there were considerable differences with regard to direction, views on knowledge, values, etc. Some of the active research personnel in the department could be said roughly to share a qualitative/'non-positivist' orientation while others were more experimentally/

quantitatively inclined. (Van Maanen and Barley (1985) speak of ideological differentiation as important in this regard.)

The concept of 'social field' stresses 'objective' features of the sameness/ differentiation theme that are not necessarily clear from the group identification or the experiences of the people involved. For example, the proponents of orthodoxy in a particular field (such as a scientific discipline) and those challenging it may not recognize that they share assumptions about the value of defending the 'right' view of science, that they all see science as an important field of activity, are interested in academic recognition, and are striving for the same types of rewards and positions. Subcultural differentiation within a field also indicates a certain degree of unity in understandings, values, and assumptions. Furthermore, there were some people in the department who were not directly connected with either research or practitioner fields. All in all, members could equally well be regarded as heterogeneous or homogeneous in terms of cultural manifestations such as values, ideals, standards, attitudes, and understandings of reality. One way of regarding dominating social and cultural patterns in the department is to regard the organization as a 'split dualism'. ('Dualism' indicates the two fields, while 'split' means that there was no homogeneity within them.)

Basically, the department was characterized by opposing competences and attitudes: the majority of those engaged in research had little connection with the most important elements in the practical-psychological field (psychotherapy and work and organizational psychology), members belonging to this field in most cases did not show much interest in research, and the Ph.D. programme, aimed at making researchers out of practitioners, was not a success. That this opposition was in no way inevitable is indicated, among other things, by the fact that the literature most read in the department (the psychoanalytic) is mainly the result of clinically based research – a synthesis of research and practitioner fields – and the combination of research and professional work is not uncommon among psychoanalysts. Members had neither the interest nor the incentive to abandon their familiar fields and expose themselves to the practical and emotional difficulties of qualifying in others that made demands on them of another kind. Furthermore, the minimization of conflict with respect to professional questions and achievements hindered confrontation between the two fields and open discussion as to what demands it was reasonable to place on university teachers of the subject, what lines of research were relevant, and so on. This avoidance of conflict can be understood in terms of the social fields and the particular organizational setting, but it is also a matter of how the actors had 'chosen' to cope with this situation or, rather, to avoid coping with it.

A more conflict-filled climate could have resulted in criticism, reappraisal, and reorganization of the local variants of the two fields. That no direct interaction and confrontation between members with different orientations took place was due in part to the strengths of the fields and in part to the somewhat uncertain identity of the majority of employees in relation to their place of employment and its task, university education in applied psychology. A doctorate was ordinarily required for university teaching, and at the same time the task demanded that teachers have considerable experience as practical psychologists. The majority of teachers had only one of these competences. Few of them, therefore, had any suitable starting point for strongly defending their own position and criticizing representatives of the other. The belief that both academic and practical competence were required for training reduced the competition between them.

Rivalry is normally most marked not between fields but within them; it is here that positions, status, privileges, and recognition are at stake (Bourdieu, 1979). For example, literary critics compete with each other, not with sports journalists. Research-oriented persons in the university normally find themselves in competition with each other and do not compete to the same extent with personnel committed to teaching or, for that matter, with persons whose main interests lie in the professional application of knowledge. Regarding the social fields which were most important in the department in question, the psychotherapeutic and the scientific fields were sharply divided with respect to what conferred status, success, etc. Competitive and conflictive elements arose between representatives of the scientific field (e.g., when they applied for the same appointment), more often than between representatives of the two different social fields.

Organizational culture and social fields

This case study suggests that it may be rewarding to distinguish between cultural conditions which apply at an overall level and those which are characteristic of social practice in which different groups are involved – between the organizational level and the different social fields to which groups within the organization belong. Organization-specific cultural manifestations and social fields exercise differential influence on individuals and consequently may be more or less salient in different situations. As a matter of fact, some of the organization's members have ideals, standards, competences, and cultural capital which, within the framework of their primary field activity, differ rather sharply from the overall patterns which distinguish the organization. In other words, there is a discrepancy between the organizational level and the individual level which, however, through its connection with social fields, is collective in character. This can, in part, be explained by the fact that at the organizational level people's values and ideals are expressed in a weak form, partly as a matter of compromise. Deep values and ideals are more strongly expressed in forms of work, these largely being connected with specific social fields rather than collective/organization-related. When, for example, it is a matter of researchers' values, these are rather clearly confined to special niches ('cultural pockets'). Examples of these were the filling of special research positions and the evaluation of publications in the department's series of research reports – matters that undoubtedly belonged to the scientific field. Here the academic-scientific field corresponded perfectly to the issues at hand and the habitus became fully appropriate. Instead of uncertainty and permissiveness, requirements and clear criteria became salient. Most of the department's activities were, however, largely immune to influence by collectively held research values.

Whereas members of the department were culturally rather heterogeneous, at the same time there were certain overall cultural understandings concerning what a member should value, believe, and think. The department displayed a certain distinct style in this respect – a certain *esprit de corps* (cf. Alvesson & Sandkull, 1988). The concept corresponds to 'corporate culture' or what I have called 'management-centric culture', and I use it here because the department essentially had no management. Its *esprit de corps* was very much a function of the negotiated social order produced by the interaction – or, rather, perhaps, the lack of genuine interaction – between the social fields for which it could be regarded as a meeting place, the practical-psychological and the (various kinds of) academic-scientific. This interaction mainly concerned the development of values and norms which reduced demands and pressures. The internal differences with respect to basic orientations and values thus contributed to a reduction of the conflict that might have brought about change. Change is otherwise said to be common in instances of differences in values and aims or organizations (e.g., Burns, 1961–62; Crozier & Friedberg, 1980; Stymne, 1970). The distance between the two social fields and the scope for different actors to pursue their private strategies without colliding with others or competing for the same resources meant, as we have seen, that no conflict-generated dynamics developed. As a negotiated social order, the department did not correspond in its boundaries to the cultures which informed many of its work activities but still produced an *esprit de corps* which affected the understandings and values of social relations and the way in which it functioned.

The department has here been described from a variety of perspectives. Considering it in its entirety, we have encountered a number of characteristic values, assumptions, standards, and orientations: caution, avoidance of making demands, a *laissez-faire* spirit, tolerance/indifference, friendliness, and a low level of conflict. This level corresponds to certain cultural manifestations broadly shared within the department which are contingent upon its history, its local actors (including the absence of leaders), its tasks, its common activities (such as the ceremony described), and the social fields and associated occupational cultures that put their imprints upon it. This organizational level is far from insignificant.

Another perspective is that of the social field, the basic competence and qualification conditions, the symbolism, the rules of the game, and the cultural codes characteristic of a certain distinct area of activity. While social fields tend to influence various personnel groups in their concrete activities, especially in those respects in which the habitus they generate provides guidelines, overall organization-related cultural patterns function as important expressions of the general social relations in the workplace. Organization-specific culture thus exists on the boundary between the individual and the collective (see, e.g., Asplund, 1983). Something similar has been noted by Dale and Spencer (1977), who found in their study of a theatre company that sentiments associated with the 'official morals' (what the organization members espoused and believed that others believed) differed from the aggregate of individual sentiments. There may be a discrepancy, then, between the values, standards, ideals, and rules for action which are publicly expressed in an organization and those held by individuals and expressed in areas of activity in which collective pressure is weak. The dominant cultural patterns in an organization may be deeply ingrained in members, but they may also be an expression of implicit negotiation, group pressure, compromise, or uncertainty.

A person assuming the existence of a unitary and unique organizational culture would have had no difficulty in finding empirical support for that view in the department. At the same time, a person believing in the existence of organizational subcultures would probably have found strong support for them. I think that this case study illustrates the fruitfulness of working with several concepts of culture – concepts of *esprit de corps* and social fields, the latter viewed in terms of both general patterns ('great culture') and the small-scale versions involved in modes of interaction ('local culture').

I will conclude this chapter by commenting upon another interpretation of culture and one which takes the issue of differentiation seriously, namely the 'ambiguity paradigm' of cultural analysis (Martin and Meyerson, 1988). (I have referred to this above, e.g. in chapter 1, and shall return to it in the next chapter.) To some extent my text is in harmony with this approach, for example in my concept of 'split dualism'. I have indicated some of the limitations of the conventional interpretation of the organization as having (or being) a single homogeneous culture or the set of distinct subcultures. Whatever cultural

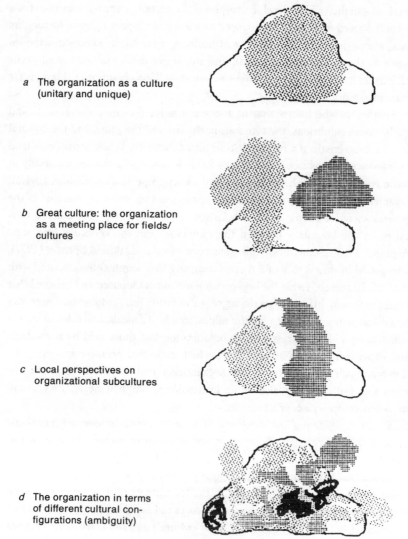

a The organization as a culture
    (unitary and unique)

b Great culture: the organization
    as a meeting place for fields/
    cultures

c Local perspectives on
    organizational subcultures

d The organization in terms
    of different cultural con-
    figurations (ambiguity)

Figure 1   Graphic illustrations of various conceptualizations of culture (ground figure = organization, patterned areas = culture)

categories we try to apply to organizational phenomena, vital elements 'slip through'. However, by using different interpretations of culture and by relating them to different kinds of phenomena, the degree of paradox, contradiction and uncertainty becomes less marked. For example the strict and almost pedantic demands of some researchers in my case study as regards publication in the department's report series, does not quite fit in with their general permissive attitude. Different types of 'cultural belongingness' – professional and organizational – account for these differences. This leads me to suspect that it might be possible to reduce the perceived ambiguity of cultural manifestations in organizations, if several 'types' of culture active in organizations were taken into consideration. (I do not believe, however, that such ambiguity can be 'explained away' in the same way.)

The approaches discussed in this chapter can be illustrated in graphical form. Figure 1a illustrates the idea of organizational culture as unitary and unique. Figure 1b portrays the social field view, proceeding from a great culture perspective in which the organization is nothing more than a passive meeting place for two social fields. Figure 1c then adopts the local perspective in which the overall cultural patterns associated with the social fields at the macro-level are played down and attention is directed towards their interaction with and impact on the local organizational context. For the sake of completeness, Figure 1d portrays the ambiguity view. My point is that the appropriateness and explanatory power of this final view is somewhat reduced if we slice the cultural pie in different ways before looking at what remains through the lens of ambiguity. Nonetheless I believe that authors who bear in mind all four ways of looking at organizational culture may be well equipped to avoid rash or unreflective conceptualizations of their research objects.

Notes

1 At the same time, I must confess that my socialization into the academic world is relatively thorough and therefore the study does not aim to illuminate broader cultural patterns which are reflected on the local level.

2 There was a third group in the department that could also have been treated at some length: lecturers who were mainly oriented to teaching and had no interest in research or application. University teaching is to a large extent dependent on either academic-scientific or practical-psychological qualifications and does not form an independent social field.

SEVEN

Beyond ambiguity

On ambiguity

Recently the idea that ambiguity is a central feature of organizational culture has become very popular. Joanne Martin and Debra Meyerson (1988), representing a broader interest in fragmentation and ambiguity, have presented an 'ambiguity paradigm' as an alternative to the two more common views on organizational culture: the integration and the differentiation paradigms. (Sköldberg, 1990, talks about a harmony and a mosaic view to signify the same perspectives.) Their work is one of the more significant contributions to organizational culture during recent years and is therefore worthy of close scrutiny.[1] Emphasis on ambiguity as a 'central feature of organizational culture' is a response to the dominance of the idea that culture is a clear and known entity that creates unity and harmony within an organization and solves problems: 'Through the development of shared meanings for events, objects, words, and people, organization members achieve a sense of commonality of experience that facilitates their coordinated action' (Smircich, 1985: 55). 'In crude relief, culture can be understood as a set of solutions devised by a group of people to meet specific problems posed by situations they face in common' (Van Maanen & Barley, 1985: 33). Schein's (1985: 149) assertion that 'all definitions of culture involve the concept of shared solutions, shared understandings, and consensus' is typical, but incorrect. Martin (1987), in contrast, points to the 'black hole' in our definitions of culture produced by the exclusion of ambiguity – uncertainty, contradiction, and confusion.

This interest in ambiguity can perhaps be seen as a reflection of the *Zeitgeist*. So-called post-modernism – which stresses uncertainty, paradox, problems of representation, etc., and can be described as 'an assault on unity' (Power, 1990) – is very popular both in social science in general (Featherstone, 1988) and in organization theory (e.g., Calás & Smircich, 1987; Cooper & Burrell, 1988). Within the more limited frame of organizational culture studies we can identify an alternation over time of rationality (here broadly defined as recognition of some logic underlying collective action) and lack of rationality. Rationalist ideas – organizational structure, contingency theory, and other examples of systems thinking – dominated up to the beginning of the 1970s. Then other types of ideas and understandings – action theory, the garbage-can theory of decision making, pluralism, power theory, and neo-Marxism – became more salient (Reed, 1985). The prevailing approaches to organizational culture have in a sense restored rationality, presenting organizational reality as following from some form of cultural logic for collective action. Peters and Waterman (1982: 51) write, for example, that 'the top performers create a broad, uplifting, shared culture, a coherent framework in which charged-up people search for appropriate adaptations. Their ability to extract extraordinary contributions from very large numbers of people turns on the ability to create a sense of highly valued purpose.' The idea of ambiguity as central, then, once again reintroduces lack of rationality. (Of course, rationalistic ideas still prevail.)

Martin and Meyerson (1988) discuss ambiguity both as what they call a paradigm – 'a subjective point of view that determines what a person perceives, conceives, and enacts as cultural' (p. 93) – and as an attribute of the research object. The distinction is very important, of course, for, as they say, different empirical contexts may encourage researchers and members of the organization to adopt different 'paradigms'. The computer consultancy company that I have referred to from time to time appears, for example, to fit what they call the 'integration paradigm', while a very hierarchical company might draw a researcher's attention to their 'differentiation paradigm'. At the same time, as they point out, 'paradigms' can be blinders, confining attention to certain aspects of culture at the expense of others: 'the ambiguity paradigm offers a distinctive view of culture, one that is centered on ambiguity itself' (p. 119). In a paper which basically attempts to apply the concept of ambiguity to empirical cases, Martin (1987) expresses the hope that 'enough evidence will be given to convince the reader that any description of these cultures that excludes ambiguities would be incomplete, misleading, and of very limited utility' (p. 5). Here empirical reality is viewed as ambiguous but capable of being described unambiguously. (This position differs, then, from that of post-modernist writers, who emphasize ambiguity also in efforts to account for research objects, in texts and language.)

I wholeheartedly agree with Martin and Meyerson that cultural studies should not equate culture with solutions, clarity, and consensus. Careful cultural research must take contradictions and uncertainties seriously, even within a cultural category, whether it is the organization, the management, the division, the occupational community, the shopfloor, or the society. I am, however, somewhat hesitant to give cultural ambiguity the prominence they accord it.

Without denying that ambiguity may 'mirror' certain features of 'objective reality' – for present purposes I do not need to address that question – I would like to show how 'evidence' of ambiguity is constructed, as all 'evidence' must be constructed, through an active process of structuring and interpreting 'reality' and then discuss other possibilities in dealing with the theme.

Ambiguity as construction

In a sense, issues of uncertainty, contradiction, and confusion could perhaps be studied just by asking people whether they are uncertain or confused. The problem is that on many (non-trivial) issues, most people are neither absolutely certain nor extremely confused. In investigating cultural ambiguity, the criteria are themselves very ambiguous. It is hardly possible to say that if x per cent of the group feels rather or very uncertain about the meaning of y per cent of a set of cultural manifestations (themselves difficult to isolate), then ambiguity is present.

A more important problem concerns the way in which culture is conceptualized. Martin and Meyerson refrain from 'offering yet another abstract definition of culture' and instead focus on what culture researchers study, including formal and informal practices, artifacts, and content themes. This means that almost anything which regularly occurs in an organization is a cultural manifestation. Most anthropologists and interpretive organizational culture researchers reject so broad a view, using the culture concept to refer to the ideational level of collectivities, that is, shared meanings, understandings, and symbols (e.g., Geertz, 1973; Keesing, 1974). Martin and Meyerson argue that most organizations are established for utilitarian purposes and therefore an understanding of economic and political considerations is inseparable from the study of organizational culture. I believe that cultural manifestations must be related to social practice but not that the concept of culture needs to include it. For me the behavioural dimension of formal and informal social practices is 'outside' culture (as an analytical category) and is best seen as part of social structure, although its meanings, understandings, and symbolism of course 'belong to' the cultural domain. It may not be easy or even necessarily fruitful to distinguish very sharply between culture and social structure, but there is, as Geertz (1973) says, some benefit in reducing the concept of culture so that it does not cover 'too much'.

Martin and Meyerson's concept of culture corresponds to a very large number of phenomena: thoughts, feelings, meanings, understandings, official policy, social structure, informal practices, rules. In fact, most of their illustrations of ambiguity are not self-evidently cultural but concern rules and procedures, limited knowledge about what is going on outside one's own level of the hierarchy and the division, criteria for promotion, etc. A more value-oriented example concerns egalitarianism in the company:

> employees are confused about [the organization's] commitment to egalitarianism. They hear relatively egalitarian rhetoric about the distribution of resources and nonfinancial rewards, open office spaces, consensual decision-making, and lateral promotions. However, their own experiences, and those of other employees, leave them confused about what the purposes of these policies are, whether these policies are desirable, how these policies are implemented, and why. (Martin & Meyerson, 1988: 115)

It seems to me, however, that confusion about rules may to some extent reflect lack of knowledge and/or structural arrangements rather than cultural ambiguity. Ambiguity is a figure (or anti-figure) that emerges against a ground of clarity, and culture emerges against a background of non-culture. The more confusion, contradiction, and uncertainty that we relate to the sphere of non-culture – contingent upon earthquakes, ignorance, structural arrangements, rapid changes in sociomaterial conditions – the less ambiguous culture appears and the less need there is for an ambiguity perspective on culture.

Martin's (1987) empirical material, partly drawing on the writings of others, is somewhat more clearly cultural in nature. One case, originally studied by Feldman (partly published in Feldman, 1991), concerns the US Department of Energy, 'a culture engulfed in ambiguity'. This organization had brought under one roof rather diverse (and partly conflicting) tasks, and changes in the political environment had created much uncertainty. The confusion was reflected in metaphors such as 'a lot of people trying to do a little bit of good – bumping into each other – all on a different wave length – with the same echo system, going crazy' and 'a combination of the Three Stooges Comedy Act, Ringling Barnum and Bailey, a three-ring circus, and five-year-olds playing in a nitroglycerine factory' (Feldman, quoted by Martin, 1987). This view seems to have been widely shared in the department, and Martin concludes that 'ambiguity is a central component of employees' experiences at this agency. Not surprisingly, then, ambiguity is central in the symbolic systems of this culture' (p. 8).

One hardly doubts that the organization was engulfed in ambiguity, but the symbolic system itself appears to be quite the opposite of ambiguous – the metaphors mentioned give a clear and rather consistent view of the organization. One gets the impression that the organization's members shared a set of understandings about the character of their workplace. These understandings were *about* ambiguous situations and conditions, but the cultural level in itself does not seem to have been characterized by confusion and uncertainty – as might have been the case if some people had referred to the department as a well-oiled machine or even as impossible to describe while others had used the metaphors just mentioned.

Again, it is not self-evident how the degree of ambiguity in an organization's culture can be assessed or, indeed, whether there is any point in drawing attention to the notion of ambiguity in the cultural understanding of organizations. (Another doubt concerns whether the concept of organizational culture is appropriate in this case – whether the department had an organizational culture.) One could in fact say that even though structural arrangements and environmental changes had created confusion, the cultural manifestations in the organization reduced the degree of uncertainty, confusion, and contradiction experienced by members – that metaphors and other symbols articulated a shared understanding and helped people anticipate and cope with ambiguity. My point is that ambiguity in structural arrangements and organizational processes does not necessarily call for (or correspond to) a perspective that focuses on ambiguity as an aspect of organizational culture. Ambiguous social structures may be accompanied by cultural meaning patterns that reflect them in a way that creates shared understandings. Thus a conventional view of culture can deal rather well with many cases of organizational ambiguity.

Uncertainty, confusion, and contradiction, are, moreover, partly a matter of how closely one looks. Cultural manifestations such as myths, rites, stories, etc., are according to most definitions ambiguous in themselves (e.g., Cohen, 1974). Even if people are, for example, familiar with a story and share attitudes to it, their interpretations of it may differ. This is to some degree inherent in cultural phenomena and not something about which most researchers are concerned on the level of the collective. On a certain level, however, ambiguity is the very stuff of cultural analysis.

The ambiguity paradigm views organizational culture in itself as ambiguous, and the more closely organizational reality is studied, the more material supporting an ambiguity view appears. Martin and Meyerson point to the ambiguity about one organization's claim to egalitarianism:

> Resources and nonfinancial rewards are supposed to be distributed at OZCO in a relatively egalitarian fashion. However, how one actually obtains a better office space, a nicer desk, or a newer computer (or any other physical object that can have status connotations) is not clear to some employees. Need, status, power and tenure all come into play, but there certainly does not seem to be a formula, even within the divisions. (1988: 113)

On a general level, the ideal of egalitarianism gives some understanding of the organization. On a more detailed level, the situation is, of course, more complicated. That certain things are not clear to 'some employees' or that egalitarianism is not the only source of particular outcomes emerges partly from a closer look at what is going on. From this example it seems that, in order not to be ambiguous, egalitarianism would have to be in almost perfect harmony with social practice and the distribution of resources would have to be transparent to nearly all employees. The criteria for avoiding the label of ambiguity are thus rather tough. And a closer look at organizational conditions leads unavoidably to the discovery of at least some elements of uncertainty, confusion and contradiction. This discovery is of course a result of adopting an ambiguity perspective, but also – and this is my point here – of careful and detailed observation.

Ambiguity in organizational culture is thus the outcome of what one is looking for and how closely one looks. (This is of course not to deny the 'influence of empirical reality' on these perception processes.) To encourage organizational culture researchers to look more closely at organizations is probably often a good thing, and I certainly agree that much of the talk about unitary, unique, and harmonious 'corporate cultures' is the result of either brief glimpses or speculation without having looked at all. Nevertheless, there are problems with a move towards much closer observation, one of which is myopia.

Cultural traffic and cultural configurations

Whereas I am favourably disposed to Martin and Meyerson's idea of ambiguity and believe that organizational culture research would benefit from considering it, I question the wisdom of focusing on ambiguity without having first carefully examined the multitude of cultures (cultural configurations) that may have left their imprints on the organizational culture in question. Even if certain phenomena cannot be understood very well in terms of a unitary organizational culture or a neatly separated set of subcultures, there are other ways of using cultural concepts to understand them. Moreover, because perceptions of ambiguity tend to come from rather detailed study, adopting this view may encourage a 'local culture' approach that excludes broader cultural patterns.

The case study in chapter 6 could easily have lent itself to interpretations based on an ambiguity view – and I believe that this view draws attention to some features of the case which could not be understood very well in any other way. But, on the whole, the combination of the concepts of culture used made it possible to understand much of what characterized the organization in terms of collectively shared understandings, meanings, symbolism, cultural capital, and cultural competence (habitus). The cultural concepts used were then not only a matter of a unitary organizational culture or a set of subcultures, but the combination of certain organizational manifestations and local versions of 'social fields' which must also be understood at the macro level. Sköldberg (1990) calls such a mixture of different and partly overlapping subcultural patterns a 'rainbow culture'. If we stay within the boundaries of the organization, cultural manifestations appear in that way, even though I prefer of course to go outside these boundaries.

In a similar way, we can also interpret one of the four illustrative cases given in Martin (1987), which has not so far been discussed here, namely the case of the Women's Bank in New York, a bank founded by women to provide services for female customers and training and jobs for female employees. Martin, referring to a dissertation by Tom, says that there was confusion about the ideological implications of working in a feminist institution, that discussion about equal opportunity was vague, and that ideological commitments provided little guidance in dealing with the apparent contradictions of working in the organization. There were two major groups in the organization; trainers, typically middle-class people, and trainees, normally with a lower-class background. Trainers were dismayed by what they saw as the 'poor' or 'unprofessional' performance of many of the trainees, for example, repeatedly failing to report to work because of sick children; instead of viewing this in terms of feminist ideology – pointing to the inadequacy of day-care centers when it comes to caring for sick children – they relied on individualistic explanations such as 'She's just not serious about wanting to work':

> From one perspective, the trainers had a point, given current norms about appropriate business behavior. On the other hand, wasn't the purpose of the bank to create an institution designed to fit the needs of female customers and employees? Bank employees could not erase the contradictions inherent in operating a feminist organization that must survive financially in a market not designed by or for feminists. (Martin, 1987: 11)

Martin concludes:

> Employees at the Women's Bank shared some understandings about how work at this bank was done. A uniquely feminist interpretation of the purpose and meaning of that work was also shared. Nevertheless, contradictions were plentiful. The bank members' commitment to feminist ideology, and the specific goal of creating an institution for and by women, failed to provide any easy resolution of these contradictions. Any description of the culture of the Women's Bank that did not include these kinds of ambiguity would be incomplete and misleading. (p. 11)

I do not disagree, but I believe that consideration of the multiple cultures represented in the case might produce a picture slightly different from the ambiguity view. The point of this view must be not only that ambiguity in the form of confusion, uncertainty, and contradiction stems from a specific integrated culture's point of view, i.e. workers deviating from top management's understanding and expectations of corporate culture, but that it also remains after 'all' the possible cultural configurations that could illuminate the phenomenon have being considered.

In the Women's Bank there were two (class-related) cultural groups which apparently had different values, understandings, and orientations. The feminist ideology of the trainers, but perhaps not always of the trainees, was strong, although even the former sometimes departed from it. Here we have some internal differentiation. Given cultural differentiation, values and ideals will be implemented to different degrees depending on the issue and the amount of influence a particular group has. Compromise, tension, and even conflict can be expected. Looking at the broader cultural situation in which the Women's Bank is situated encourages us also to take into account ideologies and values other than those held by these two groups, for example, business and work ideologies which stress competence, performance, and the work ethic. Important here, of course, as Martin says, is the pressure for financial survival, which not only gives priority to efficiency-related behaviour but also reinforces related types of understandings and values. From this perspective, what Martin interprets as ambiguity may be seen as contradiction between different cultural configurations: feminist ideology, the 'subculture' of the lower-class trainees, and the efficiency and performance-related business and work ideologies that perhaps had not been primary driving forces for the women who founded that bank but nevertheless had become salient as a result of the material situation surrounding them. In particular, one can draw attention to the salience of different female class cultures, a lower class and a middle professional class, for which work means different things. Most of what characterizes the bank can thus be interpreted as consistent with the diverse ideologies which have influenced the organization or as a result of conflicts among them.

This perspective is consistent with what Martin and Meyerson call the 'differentiation paradigm', which emphasizes conflict and inconsistencies, and because, as Martin says, there were nevertheless some broadly shared understandings what they call the 'integration paradigm' also fits the case. While I recognize that ambiguity is a central aspect of the organization, I doubt that we need a particular *paradigm* to handle it. A modification of the 'differentiation' view, especially if it is complemented with an understanding of the organization from a 'great culture' perspective, may well illuminate the contradictions in the case.

One possible way of dealing with the idea of ambiguity is to treat it as a research strategy. When ambiguity is taken as a 'paradigm' or theoretical perspective, the analysis begins and ends with it. In contrast, a research strategy concerned with ambiguity will consider it carefully with a view to resolving it, when possible, by examining the multitude of cultural configurations which influence the organization. Perceived ambiguities thus become clues to these diverse configurations. The perspective formulated here can be regarded as an alternative to the ambiguity view (as well as some other current approaches stressing fragmentation). It offers another way of dealing with contradictions in organizational cultures and functions, more like a methodology than a theoretical framework. It also serves as an alternative to the other popular views – the integration and, in particular, the differentiation views – but as a complement rather than a rival.

The perspective I am proposing can be called a *multiple cultural configuration* view. It assumes that organizations can be understood as shaping local versions of broader societal and locally developed cultural manifestations in a multitude of ways. Organizational cultures are then understandable not as unitary wholes or as stable sets of subcultures but as mixtures of cultural manifestations of different levels and kinds. People are connected to different degrees with organization, suborganizational unit, profession, gender, class, ethnic group, nation, etc.; cultures overlap in an organizational setting and are rarely manifested in 'pure' form.

It is especially important to keep in mind the existence of cultural traffic – that organizations are not cultural islands but are affected by the societal culture. In the case of my university department, in some respects people shared organizational-level understandings of social relations, but in other instances their actions were informed by the social fields to which they belonged and by their positions within those fields. In the case of the Women's Bank, a feminist ideology was broadly shared and had some influence, but on certain issues ideologies which were not organization-specific informed different members' understandings. Thus cultural configurations vary according to the issue and the ideology in question. The idea of multiple cultural configurations takes ambiguity seriously without placing it at the centre of the analysis, and opens up the possibility of 'explaining' much uncertainty, confusion, and contradiction. (In addition, I think that much ambiguity is best understood in structural terms, but that is another issue.) The multiple cultural configuration view differs from the differentiation paradigm in at least three distinct ways: (a) it focuses partly on extra-organizational origins of local cultural manifestations, without reducing these local manifestations to mere reflections of broader patterns; (b) it pays attention to overlapping cultural configurations in the organization; and (c) it sees such configurations as changing, depending on the particular issue concerned.

Prospects

This book has been an argument for a more sensitive approach to organizational culture studies. Rather than proposing a tightly integrated theoretical framework, it has attempted to stimulate reflection on a number of perspectives on culture. Studies of organizational culture move in difficult territory. Observations and analyses are very sensitive to the concepts and metaphors that inform them, and it is seldom self-evident how a given phenomenon is 'best' perceived and interpreted. It is tempting to stress complexities, and I may have succumbed to this temptation here, but I am also aware of the problems associated with demanding too much. My purpose is certainly not to discourage organizational culture research but to supplement critique with constructive ideas for addressing more interesting and socially important questions in a way that exploits the full potential of a cultural approach.

A very large part of organizational culture research has been grounded in functionalist assumptions about the potentially 'positive' consequences of culture, and has focused on founders and managers as prime movers and on instrumentally relevant cultural manifestations perceived as typical of the organization. In most such research the connection between culture, social practice, and the material aspects of people's organizational lives is neglected. In addition, the writings of many authors not very interested in 'bending' the culture concept to fit technical and instrumental preoccupations share many of these features, e.g. an idealistic focus on the organization-specific and an interest in the influence of management.

This kind of research is easy to criticize. I naturally feel that the critique introduced in the present book is on the whole fair, but consideration must be given to the purpose of management-oriented literature. What this literature does is to draw attention to the generally fairly thin, or even very thin, line of understandings, meanings, values, and symbols shared by the majority of a normal company's personnel and managers. (As has been noted there are exceptions. Sometimes the line is not so very thin. Sometimes it is not even broadly shared.) This focus is sometimes appropriate, but overlooking all the cultural manifestations which exist beyond this is counterproductive even in management's own terms. A pragmatic view of culture which can inform managerial action must to some extent consider culture's complexity; oversimplification may mislead. More important, equating organizational culture with this narrow view of it precludes use of the culture concept to raise broader questions about cultural patterns in organizations, business, and working life and diverts attention from questioning of the status quo (Casmir, 1991).

Where 'corporate culture' is in fact the research object, researchers should explicitly recognize that their approach is 'management-centric' – that they are in the business of 'thin description', concentrating on a limited but in certain respects important set of values, beliefs, meanings, and symbols, in contrast to the 'thick description' which examines complex layers of meanings in the anthropological tradition (Geertz, 1973). And, while recognizing the legitimacy and value of studies of 'management-centric culture', it can rightly be argued that the use of culture studies to call into question taken-for-granted understandings and challenge parochialism has on the whole remained underdeveloped. One reason for this, apart from the technical preoccupation just mentioned, appears to be the widespread assumption that organizations are containers of cultures and researchers need not attend to anything outside them. Equating organization and culture easily leads to myopia. Organizational culture studies would benefit from taking organizations less seriously. Geertz (1973) suggests that anthropologists do not study villages, they study *in* villages. Organizational culture researchers might benefit from reconceptualizing their projects and beginning to study *in* organizations (bearing in mind that organizations are also part of society). Cultural analysis should be permitted to move along its own tracks rather than following formal organizational lines (cf. Schneider, 1976). This is in no way inconsistent with the purpose of organizational culture research: the cultural manifestations we are talking about exist in organizational settings.

I have offered some concepts aimed at triggering constructive associations: cultural traffic, 'great culture', 'local culture', and 'management-centric culture'. The idea of multiple cultural configurations to some extent also belongs here as does my pronounced concern about the idea of organizational subcultures. This last term directs attention inwards and downwards, and away from outwards and upwards, in relation to the organization as a point of departure. The concept of social field has the advantage that it is more neutral in this regard and thus more open in some respects in terms of how to think in connection with cultural manifestations. (It has the disadvantage that it might draw attention away from the organization's setting, however, which prevents me from advocating its use too emphatically; but given the present state of the art in organization culture studies, I am not very worried about that.) As I never tire of saying, a detailed understanding of organizational culture requires careful consideration of what 'culture' means. Culture is best perceived not simply as a provider of clues for understanding social integration and harmony and guiding behaviour, but also as a theoretical tool for developing sensitivity for differentiation, inconsistency, confusion, conflict, and contradiction. Organizational culture not only serves 'positive' functions such as fulfilling people's needs for meaning, guidance, and expressiveness but also leads to closure of mind, restriction of consciousness, and reduction of autonomy. Culture provides direction but also prevents us from 'seeing'. Culture reflects and reinforces not only (true) consensus but also hegemony and domination. It is hardly possible to take all of these dimensions into account at one and the same time, but the field of study should reflect them by incorporating multiple perspectives. As Martin and Meyerson (1988: 122) put it, 'Paradigms should not be blinders. Instead, they should be thought of as a set of three lenses [integration, differentiation, and ambiguity], each one to be used in turn, again and again, in order to defocus and refocus, capturing a full view of all three aspects of any cultural context'. The adoption of various perspectives is not easy, but it is certainly not impossible, as Martin and Meyerson's and my own case studies show. As we become increasingly aware of the way in which our conceptions create understandings of reality, explicit recognition of this seems appropriate. Showing how different approaches produce partial but instructive views of cultural manifestations in organizations will hardly tell the whole story, but it can encourage reflective thinking about how organizations function and how people live their organizational lives.

Notes

1 The significance of Martin and Meyerson's framework is well illustrated by the fact that Frost *et al.*'s (1991) reader is organized in terms of it.

References

Abravanel, H. (1983) Mediatory myths in the service of organizational ideology. In Pondy, L. R. *et al.* (eds.) *Organizational Symbolism*. Greenwich, CT: JAI Press

Agar, M. H. (1986) *Speaking of Ethnography*. Beverly Hills: Sage

Ahrne, G. (1990) *Agency and Organization*. London: Sage

Allaire, Y. & Firsirotu, M. (1984) Theories of organizational culture. *Organization Studies*, 5, 193–226.

Allen, R. (1985). Four phases for bringing about cultural change. In Kilmann, R. H., Saxton, M., Serpa, R. *et al.*, *Gaining Control of Corporate Culture*. San Francisco: Jossey-Bass

Alvesson, M. (1987) *Organization Theory and Technocratic Consciousness*. Berlin/New York: de Gruyter

(1990) Organizations: From substance to image? *Organization Studies*, 11, 373–94

(1991) Organizational symbolism and ideology. *Journal of Management Studies*, 28, 3, 207–25

(1992) Leadership as social integrative action: A study of a computer consultancy company. *Organization Studies*, 13, 185–209

(1993a) *Management of Knowledge-Intensive Companies*. Berlin/New York: de Gruyter (in press)

(1993b) Cultural-ideological modes of management control. In Deetz, S. (ed.), *Communication Yearbook*, vol. 16. Newbury Park: Sage

(1993c) The play of metaphors in organizational analysis. In Parker, M. & Hassard, J. (eds.), *Postmodernism and Organisations*. London: Sage

Alvesson, M. & Berg, P. O. (1992) *Corporate Culture and Organizational Symbolism*. Berlin/New York: de Gruyter

Alvesson, M. & Billing, Y. D. (1992) Gender and organization: Toward a differentiated understanding. *Organization Studies*, 13, 73–103

Alvesson, M. & Lindkvist, L. (1993) Transaction costs, clans and corporate culture. *Journal of Management Studies*, 30, 3, 427–52

Alvesson, M. & Sandkull, B. (1988) The organizational melting-pot. An arena for different cultures. *Scandinavian Journal of Management*, 4, 135–45

Alvesson, M. & Willmott, H. (1993) *Making Sense of Management. A Critical Analysis*. London: Sage (forthcoming)

Asplund, J. (1970) *Om undran inför samhället* [On reflection on society]. Lund: Argos

(1983) *Tid, rum, individ, kollektiv* (Time, space, individual, collective). Stockholm: Liber

Baker, E. L. (1980) Managing organizational culture. *Management Review*, June 1980, 8–13

Bakka, J. F. & Fivelsdal, E. (1988) *Organisationsteori* [Organization Theory] Malmö: Liber

Barley, S. R., Meyer, G. W. & Gash, D. C. (1988) Cultures of culture: Academics, practitioners, and the pragmatics of normative control. *Administrative Science Quarterly*, 33, 24–60

Barney, J. B. (1986) Organizational culture: Can it be a source of sustained competitive advantage? *Academy of Management Review*, 11, 656–65

Bate, P. (1984) The impact of organizational culture on approaches to organizational problem-solving. *Organization Studies*, 5, 43–66

Baudrillard, J. (1983) *Simulations*. New York: Semiotext(e)

Beck, B. & Moore, L. (1985) Linking the host culture to organizational variables. In Frost, P. J. et al. (eds.), *Organizational Culture*. Beverly Hills: Sage

Beckérus, Å., Edström, A. et al. (1988) *Doktrinskiftet. Nya ideal i svenskt ledarskap*. [The Doctrine Shift. New Ideals in Swedish Management]. Stockholm: Svenska Dagbladet

Berg, P. O. (1982) 11 metaphors and their theoretical implications. In Berg, P. O. & Daudi, P. (eds.), *Traditions and Trends in Organization Theory*, part II. Lund: Studentlitteratur

(1985a) Organizational culture as a symbolic transformation process. In Frost, P. J. et al. (eds.), *Organizational Culture*. Beverly Hills: Sage

(1985b) Techno-culture: The symbolic framing of technology in a Volvo plant. *Scandinavian Journal of Management Studies*, 1, 237–56

(1986) Symbolic management of human resources. *Human Resource Management*, 25, 557–79

Berg, P. O. & Gagliardi, P. (1985) Corporate images: A symbolic perspective of the organization-environment interface. Paper presented at SCOS Conference on Corporate Images, Antibes, France June 1985

Berger, P. & Luckman, T. (1966) *The Social Construction of Reality*. New York: Anchor Books.

Bernstein, R. J. (1983) *Beyond Objectivism and Relativism*. Oxford: Basil Blackwell

Billing, Y. D. & Alvesson, M. (1993) *Gender, Managers and Organizations*. Berlin/New York: de Gruyter

Bourdieu, P. (1979) *Outline of a Theory of Practice*. Cambridge: Cambridge University Press

Boyacigiller, N. & Adler, N. (1991) The parochial dinosaur: The organizational sciences in a global context. *Academy of Management Review*, 16, 262–90

Brown, R. H. (1976) Social theory as metaphor. *Theory and Society*, 3, 169–97

Brulin, G. (1989) *Från den 'svenska modellen' till företagskorporatism?* [From the Swedish model to managerial corporatism?]. Lund: Arkiv

Burawoy, M. (1979) *Manufactoring Consent*. Chicago: University of Chicago Press

Burns, T. (1961/2) Micropolitics: Mechanisms of institutional change. *Administrative Science Quarterly*, 6, 257–81

Burrell, G. (1992) The organization of pleasure. In Alvesson, M. & Willmott, M. (eds.), *Critical Management Studies*. London: Sage

Burrell, G. & Morgan, G (1979) *Sociological Paradigms and Organizational Analysis*. London: Heinemann

Calás, M. & Smircich, L. (1987) Is the organizational culture literature dominant but dead? Paper presented at the 3rd International Conference on Organizational Symbolism and Corporate Culture, Milan, June 1987

(1988) Reading leadership as a form of cultural analysis. In Hunt, J. G. *et al.* (eds.), *Emerging Leadership Vistas*. Lexington, Mass.: Lexington Books

Calori, R. & Sarnin, P. (1991) Corporate culture and economic performance. *Organization Studies*, 12, 49–74

Casmir, F. (1991) The culture paradigm: Scholarly pursuit of knowledge and understanding or fad? Paper. Pepperdine University, Malibu, California

Clegg, S. & Dunkerly, D. (1980) *Organization, Class and Control*. London: Routledge and Kegan Paul

Cohen, A. (1974) *Two-Dimensional Man. An Essay in the Anthropology of Power and Symbolism in Complex Society*. London: Routledge and Kegan Paul

Collinson, D. (1988) 'Engineering humour': Masculinity, joking and conflict in shop-floor relations. *Organization Studies*, 9, 181–200

Cooper, R. & Burrell, G. (1988) Modernism, postmodernism and organizational analysis. *Organization Studies*, 9, 91–112

Crozier, M. & Friedberg, E. (1980) *Actors & Systems*. Chicago: University of Chicago Press

Cummings, L. L. (1984) Compensation, culture and motivation: A system perspective. *Organizational Dynamics*, 13, 1, 33–34

Czarniawska-Joerges, B. (1988a) *To Coin a Phrase. On Organizational Talk, Organizational Control and Management Consulting*. Stockholm: Stockholm School of Economics

(1988b) *Ideological Control in Nonideological Organizations*. New York: Praeger

(1992) *Exploring Complex Organizations. An Anthropological Perspective*. Newbury Park: Sage

Daft, R. (1983) Symbols in organizations. A dual-content framework for analysis. In Pondy, L. R. *et al.* (eds.), *Organizational Symbolism*. Greenwich: JAI Press

Dahlström, E. (1982) Kan sociologin förtöja kulturanalysen? [Can sociology anchor cultural analysis?]. In Hannerz, U. Liljeström, R. & Löfgren, O. (eds.), *Kultur och medvetande*. Stockholm: Akademilitteratur

Dale, A. & Spencer, L. (1977) Sentiments, norms, ideologies and myths: Their relation to the resolution of issues in a state theatre company. Working paper, EIASM, Brussels

D'Andrade, R. (1984) Cultural meaning systems. In Schweder, R. & LeVine, R. (eds.), *Culture Theory*. Cambridge: Cambridge University Press

Dandridge, T. C. (1986) Ceremony as the integration of work and play. *Organization Studies*, 7, 159–70

Dandridge, T. C., Mitroff, I. I. & Joyce, W. F. (1980) Organizational symbolism: a topic to expand organizational analysis. *Academy of Management Review*, 5, 77–82

Davis, T. (1985) Managing culture at the bottom. In Kilmann, R. H., Saxton, M., Serpa, R. *et al.* (1985) *Gaining Control of Corporate Culture*. San Francisco: Jossey-Bass

Deal, T. E. & Kennedy, A. A. (1982) *Corporate Culture*. Reading: Addison-Wesley

Deetz, S. (1985) Ethical considerations in cultural research in organizations. In Frost, P. J. *et al.* (eds.), *Organizational Culture*. Newbury Park: Sage

(1992) *Democracy in an Age of Corporate Colonization*. Albany: State University of New York Press

Deetz, S. & Kersten, S. (1983) Critical models of interpretive research. In Putnam, L. & Pacanowsky, M. (Eds.), *Communication and Organizations*. Beverly Hills: Sage

Denison, D. (1984) Bringing corporate culture to the bottom line. *Organizational Dynamics*, 13, 2, 4–22

Ehn, B. & Löfgren, O. (1982) *Kulturanalys* [Cultural analysis]. Lund: Liber

Etzioni, A. (1988) *The Moral Dimension*. New York: Free Press

Featherstone, M. (1988) In pursuit of the postmodern: An introduction. *Theory, Culture & Society*, 5, 195–215

Feldman, J. (1991) The meaning of ambiguity: Learning from stories and metaphors. In Frost, P. J. *et al.* (eds.) *Reframing Organizational Culture*. Newbury Park: Sage

Feldman, J. & March, J. (1981) Information in organizations as signal and symbol, *Administrative Science Quarterly*, 26, 171–86

Fitzgerald, T. (1988) Can change in organizational culture really be managed? *Organizational Dynamics*, 17, 2, 4–15

Foley, D. (1989) Does the working class have a culture in the anthropological sense? *Cultural Anthropology*, 137–62

Fombrun, C. (1986) Structural dynamics within and between organizations. *Administrative Science Quarterly*, 31, 403–21

Forester, J. (1983) Critical theory and organizational analysis. In Morgan, G. (ed.), *Beyond Method*. Beverly Hills: Sage

Foucault, M. (1980) *Power/Knowledge*. New York: Pantheon

Frost, P. J. (1987) Power, politics, and influence. In Jablin, F. *et al.* (eds.) *Handbook of Organizational Communication*. Newbury Park: Sage

Frost, P. J. *et al.* (eds.) (1985) *Organizational Culture*. Newbury Park: Sage

(1991) *Reframing Organizational Culture*. Newbury Park: Sage

Gagliardi, P. (1986) The creation and change of organizational cultures: A conceptual framework. *Organizational Studies*, 7, 117–34

(1990) Artifacts as pathways and remains of organizational life. In Gagliardi, P. (ed.), *Symbols and Artifacts: Views of the Corporate Landscape*. Berlin/New York: de Gruyter

(1991) Organizational anthropology, organization theory, and management practice. Paper presented at the 8th SCOS conference, Copenhagen, June 1991

Gardell, B. (1976) *Arbetsinnehåll och livskvalitet*. [Work content and quality of life]. Stockholm: Prisma

Geertz, C. (1973) *The Interpretation of Culture*. New York: Basic Books

Giesen, B. & Schmid, M. (1989) Symbolic, institutional, and social-structural differentiation: A selection-theoretical perspective. In Haferkamp, H. (ed.), *Social Structure and Culture*. Berlin/New York: de Gruyter

Goffman, E. (1961) *Asylums*. Garden City: Doubleday

Gregory, K. L. (1983) Native-view paradigms. Multiple cultures and culture conflicts in organizations. *Administrative Science Quarterly*, 28, 359–76

Gusfield, J. & Michalowicz, J. (1984) Secular symbolism: Studies of ritual, ceremony and the symbolic order in modern life. *Annual Review of Sociology*, 10, 417–35

Habermas, J. (1970) On systematically distorted communication. *Inquiry*, 13, 205–18 (1972) *Knowledge and Human Interests*. London: Heinemann

Hackmann, J. R. *et al.* (1975) A new strategy for job enrichment. In Staw, B. (ed.), *Psychological Foundations of Organizational Behaviour*. Santa Monica: Goodyear

Hannerz, U. (1988) Culture between center and periphery: Toward a macroanthropology. Paper presented at symposium on Culture in Complex Societies, Stockholm, April 1988

Helmers, S. (1991) Anthropological contributions to organizational culture. *SCOS Notework*, 10, 60–72

Hofstede, G. (1985) The interaction between national and organizational value systems. *Journal of Management Studies*, 22, 347–57

Hofstede, G., Neuijen, D., Ohayv, D. & Sanders, G. (1990) Measuring organizational cultures: A qualitative and quantitative study across twenty cases. *Administrative Science Quarterly*, 35, 286–316

Horkheimer, M. & Adorno, T. (1947) *The Dialectics of Enlightenment*. London: Verso 1979

Jackson, N. & Willmott, H. (1987) Beyond epistemology and reflective conversation: Towards human relations. *Human Relations*, 40, 361–80

Jeffcutt, P. (1991) From interpretation to representation in organisational analysis: Post-modernism, ethnography and organisational culture. Paper presented at the 'Towards a New Theory of Organization' conference, Keele University, April 1991

Johansson, O. L. (1990) *Organisationsbegrepp och begreppsmedvetenhet.* [Concepts of organization and conceptual awareness]. Göteborg: BAS

Jones, G. (1983) Transaction costs, property rights and organizational culture: An exchange perspective. *Administrative Science Quarterly*, 28, 454–57

Kanter, R. M. (1983) *The Change Masters*. London: Unwin-Hyman

Karasek, R. A. (1981) Job socialization and stress. In Gardell, B. & Johansson, G. (eds.), *Working Life*. Chichester: Wiley

Keesing, R. (1974) Theories of culture, *Annual Review of Anthropology*, 3, 73–97

Kernberg, O. (1980) Organizational regression. In *Internal World and External Reality*. New York: Jason Aronson

Kets de Vries, M. & Miller, D. (1984) *The Neurotic Organization*. San Francisco: Jossey-Bass
  (1986) Personality, culture and organization. *Academy of Management Review*, 11, 266–79

Kilmann, R. H. (1985) Five steps to close the culture gap. In Kilmann, R. H., Saxton, M., Serpa, R. *et al.*, *Gaining Control of Corporate Culture*. San Francisco: Jossey-Bass

Kilmann, R. H., Saxton, M., Serpa, R. *et al.* (1985) *Gaining Control of Corporate Culture*. San Francisco: Jossey-Bass

Knights, D. & Willmott, H. C. (1987) Organizational culture as management strategy: A critique and illustration from the financial service industries. *International Studies of Management & Organization*, 17, 3, 40–63

Knorr-Cretina, K. (1981) Introduction. The micro-sociological challenge of macro-sociology: Towards a reconstruction of social theory and methodology. In Knorr-

Cetina, K. & Cicourel, A. (eds.), *Advances in Social Theory and Methodology*. Boston: Routledge and Kegan Paul

Kohn, M. (1980) Job complexity and adult personality. In Smelser, N. & Erikson, E. H. (eds.), *Themes of Work and Love in Adulthood*. Cambridge, Mass: Harvard University Press

Krefting, L. & Frost, P. J. (1985) Untangling webs, surfing waves, and wildcatting: A multiple-metaphor perspective on managing organizational culture. In Frost, P. J. *et al.* (eds.), *Organizational Culture*, Beverly Hills: Sage

Kuhn, T. S. (1970). *The Structure of Scientific Revolutions*. Chicago: University of Chicago Press.

Kunda, G. (1991). Ritual and management of corporate culture. A critical perspective. Paper presented at the 8th International SCOS Conference, Copenhagen, June 1991

Kunda, G. & Barley, S. R. (1988) Designing devotion: Corporate culture and ideologies of workplace control. Paper presented at the American Sociological Association 83rd Annual Meeting, Atlanta, August 1988

Lakoff, G. & Johnsson, M. (1980) *Metaphors We Live By*. Chicago: University of Chicago Press

Lasch, C. (1978) *The Culture of Narcissism*. New York: Norton

Laurent, A. (1978) Managerial subordinacy: A neglected aspects of organizational hierarchy. *Academy of Management Review*, 3, 220–30

Leach, E. (1982) *Social Anthropology*. Glasgow: Fontana

LeVine, R. (1984) Properties of culture: An ethnographic view. In Shweder, R. & LeVine, R. (eds.), *Culture Theory*. Cambridge: Cambridge University Press

Linstead, S. (1985) Symbolization and ambiguity in organizations: Induction, humour, and the symbolic process. *CEBES journal*, 1, 2, 52–97

Linstead, S. & Grafton-Small, R. (1990) Theory as artefact: Artefact as theory. In Gagliardi, P. (ed), *Symbols and Artifacts: Views of the Corporate Landscape*. Berlin/New York: de Gruyter

Löfgren, O., (1982) Kulturbygge och kulturkonfrontation [Culture building and culture confrontation]. In Hannerz, U., Liljeström, R. & Löfgren, O. (eds.), *Kultur och medvetande*. Stockholm: Akademilitteratur

Louis, M. R. (1980) Surprise and sense-making: What newcomers experience in entering unfamiliar organizational settings. *Administrative Science Quarterly*, 25, 226–51

(1981) A culture perspective on organizations: The need for and consequences of viewing organizations as cultural-bearing milieux. *Human Systems Management*, 2, 246–58

(1985) An investigator's guide to workplace culture. In Frost, P. J. *et al.* (eds.), *Organizational Culture*. Beverly Hills: Sage

Lundberg, C. C. (1985) On the feasibility of cultural intervention in organizations. In Frost, P. J. *et al.* (eds.), *Organizational Culture*, Beverly Hills: Sage

Mangham, I. & Overington, M. (1987) *Organizations as Theatre*. Chichester: Wiley

March, J. & Olsen, J. (1976) *Ambiguity and Choice in Organizations*, Bergen: Universitetsforlaget

Marcus, G. & Fischer, M. (1986) *Anthropology as Cultural Critique*. Chicago: University of Chicago Press

Marcuse, H. (1964) *One-dimensional Man*. Boston: Beacon Press
  (1968) *Negations*. Harmondsworth: Penguin
Martin, H. (1985) Managing specialized corporate cultures. In Kilmann, R. H., Saxton, M. Serpa, R. *et al.* (1985) *Gaining Control of Corporate Culture*, San Francisco: Jossey-Bass
Martin, J. (1987) The Black Hole. Ambiguity in organizational cultures. Paper presented to the 3rd International Conference on Organization Symbolism and Corporate Culture, Milan, June 1987
Martin, J., Feldman, M. S. Hatch, M. J. & Sitkin, S. B. (1983) The uniqueness paradox in organizational stories. *Administrative Science Quarterly*, 28, 438–53
Martin, J. & Meyerson, D. (1988) Organizational cultures and the denial, channeling and acknowledgement of ambiguity. In Pondy, L. R. *et al.* (eds.), *Managing Ambiguity and Change*. New York: Wiley
Martin, J. & Siehl, C. (1983) Organizational culture and counter culture: An uneasy symbiosis. *Organizational Dynamics*, 12, Autumn, 52–64
Martin, J. Sitkin, S. & Boehm, M. (1985) Founders and the elusiveness of a cultural legacy. In Frost, P. J. *et al.* (eds.) *Organizational Culture*. Beverly Hills: Sage
Masterman, M. (1970) The nature of a paradigm. In Lakatos, I. & Musgrave, A. (eds.), *Criticism and the Growth of Knowledge*. Cambridge: Cambridge University Press.
Menzies, I. (1960) A case study in the functioning of social systems as a defence against anxiety. *Human Relations*, 13, 95–121
Meyerson, D. & Martin, J. (1987) Cultural change: An integration of three different views. *Journal of Management Studies*, 24, 623–48
Mills, A. (1988) Organization, gender and culture. *Organization Studies*. 9, 351–70
Mintzberg, H. (1983) *Structure in fives. Designing effective organizations*. Englewood Cliffs, NJ: Prentice-Hall
Molstad, C. (1989) The shopfloor culture of California industrial brewery workers: Leadership via expertise, impression management and rhetoric. Paper presented at The Fourth International Conference on Organizational Symbolism and Corporate Culture, INSEAD, 28–30 June 1989
Morey, N. & Luthans, F. (1985) Refining the concept of culture and the use of scenes and themes in organizational studies. *Academy of Management Review*, 10, 219–29
Morgan, G. (1980) Paradigms, metaphors, and puzzle solving in organizational analysis. *Administrative Science Quarterly*, 25, 606–22
  (1983). More on metaphor: Why we cannot control tropes in administrative science. *Administrative Science Quarterly*, 28, 601–8
  (1986) *Images of Organization*. Beverly Hills: Sage
Morgan, G., Frost, P. J. and Pondy, L. R. (1983) Organizational symbolism. In Pondy, L. R. *et al.* (eds.), *Organizational Symbolism*. Greenwich, CT: JAI Press
Mumby, D. (1988) *Communication and Power in Organizations: Discourse, Ideology and Domination*. Norwood, NJ: Ablex
Nord, W. (1985) Can organized culture be managed? A synthesis. In Frost, P. J. *et al.* (eds.), *Organizational Culture*. Beverly Hills: Sage
Ortner, S. (1973) On key symbols. *American Anthropologist*, 75, 1338–46

(1984) Theory in anthropology since the sixties. *Comparative Studies in Society and History*, 26, 126–66

Österberg, D. (1971) *Makt och materiell* [Power and materia]. Göteborg: Korpen

(1985) Materiell och praxis [Materia and praxis]. In Anderson, S. *et al.*, *Mellan människor och ting*. Göteborg: Korpen

Ouchi, W. G. (1980). Markets, bureaucracies and clans, *Administrative Science Quarterly*, 25, 129–41

(1981) *Theory Z*. Reading: Addison-Wesley

Ouchi, W. G. & Wilkins, A. L. (1985) Organizational culture. *Annual Review of Sociology*, 11, 457–83

Outhwaite, W. (1983) Toward a realist perspective. In Morgan, G. (ed.), *Beyond Method*. Beverly Hills, Sage

Pacanowsky, M. & O'Donnell-Trujillo, N. (1983) Organizational communication as cultural performance. *Communication Monographs*, 50, 126–47

Pascale, R. T. (1985) Reconciling ourselves to socialization. *California Management Review*, 27,1, 26–41

Pennings, H. & Gresov, C. (1986) Techno-economic and structural correlates of organizational culture: an integrative framework. *Organization Studies*, 7, 317–34

Perrow, C. (1986) *Complex Organizations: A Critical Essay* (3rd ed.). New York: Random House

Peters, T. J. & Waterman, R. H. (1982) *In Search of Excellence*. New York: Harper and Row

Pettigrew, A. (1979) On studying organizational cultures. *Administrative Science Quarterly*, 24, 570–81

(1985) Examining change in the long-term context of culture and politics. In Pennings, J. *et al.* (eds.) *Organizational Strategy and Change*. San Francisco: Jossey-Bass

Pfeffer, J. (1981) Management as symbolic action: The creation and maintenance of organizational paradigms. In Cummings, L. L., Staw, B. M. (eds.), *Research in Organizational Behaviour*, vol. 3. Greenwich, CT: JAI Press

Pfeffer, J. & Salancik, G. (1978) *The External Control of Organizations*. New York: Harper & Row

Pinder, C. & Bourgeois, V. (1982) Controlling tropes in administrative science. *Administrative Science Quarterly*, 27, 641–52

Pondy, L. R. (1983) The role of metaphors and myths in organizations and in the facilitation of change. In Pondy, L. R. *et al.* (eds.), *Organizational Symbolism*. Greenwich: JAI Press

Power, M. (1986) Modernism, postmodernism and organisation. Papers presented at International Workshop on Aspects on Organisation, University of Lancaster, January 1986

Putnam, L. (1983) The interpretive perspective: An alternative to functionalism. In Putnam, L. & Pacanowsky, M. (eds.), *Communication and Organization*. Beverly Hills: Sage

Putnam, L. & Pacanowsky, M. (eds.) (1983), *Communication and Organization*. Beverly Hills: Sage

Ranson, S., Hinings, C. R. & Greenwood, R. (1980) The structuring of organizational structures. *Administrative Science Quarterly*, 25, 1–17

Ray, C. A. (1986) Corporate culture: The last frontier of control. *Journal of Management Studies*, 23, 3, 287–96

Reed, M. (1985) *Redirections in Organizational Analysis*. London: Tavistock
    (1990) From paradigms to images: The paradigm warrior turns post-modern guru. *Personnel Review*, 19, 3, 35–40

Ricoeur, P. (1978) Metaphor and the main problem of hermeneutics. In *The Philosophy of Paul Ricoeur*. Boston: Beacon Press

Rosen, M. (1985) Breakfirst at Spiro's: Dramaturgy and dominance. *Journal of Management*, 11, 2, 31–48
    (1988) You asked for it: Christmas at the bosses' expense. *Journal of Management Studies*, 25, 463–80

Saffold, G. S. (1988) Culture traits, strength, and organizational performance: Moving beyond "strong" culture. *Academy of Management Review*, 13, 546–58

Sathe, V. (1983) Implications of corporate culture: A manager's guide to action. *Organizational Dynamics*, 12, Autumn, 5–23
    (1985) How to decipher and change organizational culture. in Kilmann, R. H., *et al.* (eds.), *Gaining Control of the Corporate Culture*. San Francisco: Jossey-Bass

Schein, E. H. (1985) *Organizational Culture and Leadership*. San Francisco: Jossey-Bass

Schneider, D. (1976) Notes toward a theory of culture. In Baso, K. & Selby, H. (eds.), *Meaning in Anthropology*. Albuquerque: University of New Mexico Press

Schön, D. (1979) Generative metaphor: A perspective on problem-setting in social policy. In Ortony, A. (ed.), *Metaphor*. Cambridge: Cambridge University Press

Schwartz, H. S. (1988) The symbol of the Space Shuttle and the degeneration of the American dream. *Journal of Organizational Change Management*, 1, 2, 5–20

Sennett, R. (1980) *Authority*. New York: Vintage Books

Siehl, C. (1985) After the founder: An opportunity to manage culture. In Frost, P. J. *et al.* (eds.), *Organizational Culture*. Beverly Hills: Sage

Siehl, C. & Martin, J. (1990) Organizational culture: A key to financial performance? In Schneider, B., (ed.), *Organizational Culture and Climate*. San Francisco: Jossey-Bass

Sköldberg, K. (1990) *Administrationens poetiska logik*. Lund: Student-litteratur

Smircich, L. (1983a) Concepts of culture and organizational analysis. *Administrative Science Quarterly*, 28, 339–58
    (1983b) Studying organizations as cultures. In Morgan, G. (ed.), *Beyond Method*. Beverly Hills: Sage
    (1983c) Organizations as shared meanings. In Pondy, L. R. *et al.* (eds.) *Organizational Symbolism*. Greenwich: JAI Press
    (1985) Is organizational culture a paradigm for understanding organizations and ourselves? In Frost, P. J. *et al.* (eds.) *Organizational Culture*. Beverly Hills: Sage

Smircich, L. & Morgan, G. (1982) Leadership: The management of meaning. *Journal of Applied Behavioural Science*, 18, 257–73

Smircich, L. & Stubbart, C. (1985) Strategic management in an enacted world. *Academy of Management Review*, 10, 724–36

Stablein, R. & Nord, W. (1985) Practical and emancipatory interests in organizational symbolism. *Journal of Management*, 11, 2, 13–28

Stymne, B. (1970) *Values and Processes*. Lund: Studentlitteratur

Sulkunen, P. (1982) Society made visible – on the cultural sociology of Pierre Bourdieu. *Acta Sociologica*, 25, 103–16

Sunesson, S. (1981) *När man inte lyckas* [When you don't succeed]. Stockholm: AWE/ Gebers

Swidler, A. (1986) Culture in action: Symbols and strategies. *American Sociological Review*, 51, 273–86

Sypher, B. D., Applegate, J. & Sypher, H. (1985) Culture and communication in organizational contexts. In Gudykunst, W. *et al.* (eds.), *Communication, Culture and Organizational Processes*, Beverly Hills: Sage

Tepperman, J. (1976) Organizing office workers. *Radical America*, 10, 1

Tinker, T. (1986) Metaphor or reification: Are radical humanists really libertarian anarchists? *Journal of Management Studies*, 25, 363–84

Tompkins, P. (1987) Translating organizational theory: Symbolism over substance. In Jablin, F. *et al.*, (eds.), *Handbook of Organizational Communication*. Newbury Park: Sage

Trice, H. M. & Beyer, J. M. (1984) Studying organizational cultures through rites and ceremonies. *Academy of Management Review*, 9, 653–69

(1985) Using six organizational rites to change culture. In Kilmann, R. H. *et al.*, *Gaining Control of the Corporate Culture*. San Francisco: Jossey-Bass

Trist, E. & Bamforth, K. (1951) Some social and psychological consequences of the longwall method of coal-getting. In Pugh, D. (ed.), *Organization Theory*. Harmondsworth: Penguin Books 1984

Tsoukas, H. (1991) Analogies and metaphors in organisation theory: A critical review. Paper presented at the 'Towards a New Theory of Organization' conference, Keele University, April 1991

Turner, B. (1971) *Exploring the Industrial Subculture*. London: Macmillan

Van Maanen, J. & Barley, S. R. (1984) Occupational communities: Culture and control in organizations. In Staw, B. M. & Cummings, L. L. (eds.), *Research in Organizational Behaviour*, vol., 6. Greenwich: JAI Press

(1985) Cultural organization. Fragments of a theory. In Frost, P. J. *et al.* (eds.), *Organizational Culture*. Beverly Hills: Sage

Van Maanen, J. & Kunda, G. (1989) Real feelings: Emotional expression and organizational culture. In Staw, B. M. & Cummings, L. L. (eds.), *Research in Organizational Behaviour*, vol., 11. Greenwich: JAI Press

Van Maanen, J. & Schein, E. H. (1979) Towards a theory of organizational socialization. In Staw, B. (ed.), *Research in Organizational Behaviour*, Greenwich: JAI Press

Weick, K. E. (1987) Theorizing about organizational communication. In Jablin, F. *et al.* (eds.), *Handbook of Organizational Communication*. Newbury Park: Sage

Westlander, G. (1976) *Arbete och fritidssituation* [The work and leisure Situation]. Stockholm: PA-rådet

Westley, F. & Jaeger, A. (1985) An examination of organizational culture: How is it linked to performance? Paper, Faculty of Management, McGill University, Montreal

Whipp, R., Rosenfeld, R. & Pettigrew, A. (1989) Culture and competitiveness: Evidence from two mature industries. *Journal of Management Studies*, 26, 6, 561–85

Wiener, Y. (1988) Forms of value systems: A focus on organizational effectiveness and cultural change and maintenance. *Academy of Management Review*, 13, 534–45

References

Wilkins, A. L. (1983) Organizational stories as symbols which control the organization. In Pondy, L. R. *et al.* (eds.) *Organizational Symbolism*. Greenwich: JAI Press

Wilkins, A. L. & Dyer, W. G. (1987) Toward a theory of culture change: A dialectic and synthesis. Paper presented at the 3rd International Conference on Organizational Symbolism and Corporate Culture, Milan, June 1987

Wilkins, A. L. & Ouchi, W. G. (1983) Efficient cultures: Exploring the relationship between culture and organizational performance. *Administrative Science Quarterly*, 28, 468–81

Wilkins, A. L. & Patterson, K. (1985) You can't get there from here: What will make culture-change projects fail. In Kilmann, R. H., Saxton, M., Serpa, R. *et al.*, *Gaining Control of Corporate Culture*. San Francisco: Jossey-Bass

Willmott, H. (1991) Strength is ignorance; slavery is freedom: Managing culture in modern organizations. Paper presented at the 8th International Conference on Organizational Symbolism, Copenhagen

von Wright, G. H. (1986) *Vetenskapen och förnuftet* [Science and reason]. Stockholm: Månpocket

Young, E. (1989) On the naming of the rose: Interests and multiple meanings as elements of organizational culture. *Organization Studies*, 10, 187–206

Ziehe, T. & Stubenrauch, H. (1982) *Plädoyer für ungewöhnliches Lernen. Ideen zur Jugendsituation*. Hamburg: Rowholt Taschenbuch

Index

Abravanel, H., 63
academic-scientific field, in a university
    department, 102–5, 106
acquisitions, and organizational culture, 36, 37
action theory, 111
Adler, N., 47, 54
Adorno, T., 27, 48, 54
affect-regulator, culture as, 21, 25
Agar, M. H., 53
Ahrne, G., 93
Allaire, Y., 16, 41, 96
Alvesson, M., 3, 4, 15, 18, 29, 30, 31, 44, 46,
    48, 52, 55, 57, 61, 71, 71–2, 75, 89, 106
    study of consultancy company, 71–2, 86–7,
    89, 111
ambiguity, 7, 21–2
    and cultural analysis, 107–9, 110–21
anthropology, and organizational culture, 66
anxiety-producing work, 68–9
Applegate, J., 43
Aristotle, 10
Asplund, J., 53, 107

Baker, E. L., 28
Bakka, J. F., 85
Bamforth, K., 38
Barley, S. R., 4–5, 35, 40, 67, 75, 76, 89, 104,
    110
Barney, J. B., 29
Baudrillard, J., 54
Beck, B., 79, 81
Beckérus, A., 4
Berg, P. O., 3, 4, 11, 30, 31, 33, 62, 74
Berger, P., 34
Bernstein, R. J., 26
Beyer, J. M., 20–1, 26, 28, 47, 60, 61, 64, 65,
    88, 96
Billing, Y. D., 55
blinders
    culture as, 22–3, 25, 26
    paradigms as, 111, 121
Boehm, M., 24

Boston Consulting Group, 5
Bourdieu, P., 47, 101, 102, 105
Bourgeois, V., 9, 10, 12
Boyacigillar, N., 47, 54
Brown, R. H., 10, 11, 17
Brulin, G., 4
Burawoy, M., 68, 80
bureaucracy, and organizational culture, 39,
    45, 61, 67–8
Burns, T., 106
Burrell, G., 1, 5, 14, 24–5, 110

Calás, M., 11, 64, 110
Calori, R., 40
career filters, 76
careerism, and parochialism, 56
Casmir, F., 119
ceremonies
    organizational, 61
    and social practices, 71
    in a university department, 96–100
change
    cultural, 3; instrumental and normative bias
    in, 28–9
    social, 70
Christmas parties, 60, 61, 71
Clegg, S., 55
closed organization climate, 89
cognition, and metaphors for culture, 25
Cohen, A., 72, 114
collective competence, 28
Collinson, D., 68
commitment, symbols of, 61
communication distortions, in organizations,
    55
compass, culture as, 18–19, 20, 25, 26
competitive advantage, and organizational
    culture, 29
conflict
    intergroup, 38
    rites in conflict reduction, 65
    in a university department, 95, 106–7